Cancel the Pity Party

✦

Five Steps to Creating Your Best Life

Lita Rawdin Singer, Ph.D.

*With Stephanie Dawn Singer, MS
and Brandon Singer*

ⓔiUniverse®

CANCEL THE PITY PARTY
FIVE STEPS TO CREATING YOUR BEST LIFE

iUniverse books may be ordered through booksellers or by contacting:

iUniverse
1663 Liberty Drive
Bloomington, IN 47403
www.iuniverse.com
1-800-Authors (1-800-288-4677)

Because of the dynamic nature of the Internet, any web addresses or links contained in this book may have changed since publication and may no longer be valid. The views expressed in this work are solely those of the author and do not necessarily reflect the views of the publisher, and the publisher hereby disclaims any responsibility for them.

Any people depicted in stock imagery provided by Thinkstock are models, and such images are being used for illustrative purposes only. Certain stock imagery © Thinkstock.

ISBN: 978-1-4917-6039-0 (sc)
ISBN: 978-1-4917-6041-3 (hc)
ISBN: 978-1-4917-6040-6 (e)

Library of Congress Control Number: 2015902197

Print information available on the last page.
Printed in the United States of America.

iUniverse rev. date: 02/23/2015

To my parents,
children and grandchildren,
teachers, students, and patients

The two most important days of your life
are the day you were born
and the day you found out why.

—Mark Twain

Contents

Acknowledgments

I am deeply grateful to many people who contributed in different ways to the evolution of this book and its concepts. I am especially grateful to my teachers who gave me not only the positive contributions but also the many challenges. The challenges were the greatest gift, for they kept me on my quest to know and to be the perennial student.

I want to thank my patients and students who have opened themselves to me and raised provoking questions and challenged my ideas. All of the people in the book are constructed composites based on my four decades of clinical practice. In all cases, I have changed names as well as other identifying details in order to protect privacy.

I am deeply grateful to Donald Meichenbaum, whose work in the field of cognitive behavioral therapy has been my foundation. His wisdom, knowledge, generosity, and sense of humor have been my strength and support, and I am thankful to have known him. I am also deeply grateful to the works of Viktor Frankl, and I'm pleased to have met him in his ninetieth year, at a conference in Germany. We grow on the shoulders of the others who have come before us, and I am eternally grateful for all I have been fortunate enough to experience.

I thank my family. I especially thank my daughter Stephanie for all she has added to this book and for the knowledge she has shared from her work with biofeedback, neurofeedback, and psychotherapy. Also, thanks for the work and contribution of my grandson Brandon Singer on biofeedback and psychotherapy.

I thank Robin Quinn for her work in editing the book and for her keen eye and vision. Also, I want to thank those at iUniverse who have worked hard to get this project completed.

I am most grateful to all of my sources of great inspiration, including Fariba, my poetry teacher; the poetry of Rumi; and the teachings of the Buddha. Most of all, I am deeply grateful for the guidance of the spirit within, without which this never could have been done.

Introduction

We have within us the energy to thrive and to flourish; to find out our purpose, our truth; and to leave this world in better shape than we found it. Sometimes we are able to access this energy, and other times, we are not.

When we tap into this energy, we feel energized and excited by new ideas; connected to and loved by others; and physically healthy, emotionally clear, and purposefully productive. It is at these times when we feel at one with the universe and at peace within. Going through the five steps in the book will guide you to this place.

So what does it mean to "cancel the pity party"? Well, it is a solitary exercise for someone to feel sorry for him- or herself. Those victims who throw a pity party bemoan their fates, comparing themselves to people who are richer, smarter, thinner, funnier, sexier, and better looking. *Oh, woe is me!* Blaming everyone and everything for their unhappiness, they are negative about most, if not all, parts of their lives. These folks moan and groan and find reasons to be miserable. In fact, they seem to like feeling down. They gain attention from being sick, sad, depressed, hurt, victimized, and mistreated. The more they look for reasons for their misery, the more they find them. These reasons pile up like a mountain, proving to everyone that the victims' lives are hard, they're right to be miserable, and they're justified in feeling sorry for themselves.

I often see these kinds of patients in therapy. They're not in that energized state of being I described above. Instead, they have lost their inner vision, power, purpose, self-love, and inner peace.

After forty years as a therapist and much time spent as a psychology professor, a supervisor of other therapists and interns, a citizen of the world, a wife, a mother, and a grandmother, I have learned the lessons and experienced the journey necessary to get to that place of inner peace. The process involves first recognizing your problems. Then, rather than complain, whine, and wallow in negativity, you learn to find solutions. *You* become the solution, developing new ways of thinking, feeling, and behaving until this new mind-set becomes a habit. With time, you change your life.

Life and stuff happen—bad things happen. Learn to deal with it! Stop feeding the misery beast. You—and *only you*—have the power to decide how you're going to feel about your life. It's possible to construct a new story for yourself.

The Journey

Using the five steps in this book, you will undertake a journey of exploration of your inner self. You will turn to the one expert who, for every moment of every day of your existence, has been collecting the data necessary to finally get to your goal. That expert is you!

In working with the book, you will be exploring your intuitive experience—what it's like to be you. You will be seeking your direct experience. The great news is that you can't fail at this, because your self is what you are at all times and in all places. You simply need to sort yourself out.

The steps in this book are mirrors to help you see yourself from different angles. Although the journey is an inner one, it will draw upon every aspect of your life. The only requirement is your willingness to look honestly at yourself in the most natural, intuitive manner.

As you go through this journey, you'll find that you know much more about yourself than you thought you did. The fact is that you already know how to find yourself, but you've gotten distracted and disoriented. Once you're refocused, you will realize that you have the ability to not only find yourself but also free yourself. Whether you choose to do so or not is entirely up to you. But if you go far enough on this journey, there will be no more confusion, lack of empowerment, or blaming others. You'll know what has to be done, and should you choose to devote yourself to the ongoing journey within, you will develop a tremendous sense of respect for who you really are.

The Steps

You have the choice to proceed on this journey by following the steps listed below. If you choose not to take this journey and don't want to do the work, then return the book to the shelf or close it on your e-reader. "Leave this gathering," as the poet and mystic Rumi says. Continue the pity party, and continue to be the victim.

However, it is my hope that you will decide to start your journey. Let's go!

It starts with step one: mind. Every day, we confront an endless, swirling, changing flow of scenes and situations. How does your mind make sense of the world and all of this information? The latest research points to analogy. Our brains are mighty analogy machines, endlessly linking this to that and that to the other. The five senses bring in the data. This book will help you sort out how you create your world and your story with this information that comes in through your senses—taste, sight, sound, touch, and smell. You will also receive supportive tools to use as you create a new story and develop your optimal self.

Next is step two: body. In this chapter, you will learn about how to self-regulate to help keep yourself calm and to deal with the stresses that life presents. In addition, you'll see how using biofeedback can help you become mindful and conscious of how to achieve the skills you need. (Biofeedback is a process through which you can learn to use feedback from electronic monitoring of your body's responses in your personal growth.) You will also learn how your environment has an important impact on your physical being.

Step number three is the brain. Even if you're stressed out, depressed, compulsive, or anxious right now, it is possible for you to learn to fully access your cognitive and intellectual abilities. Neurofeedback can assist you in staying focused and using your brain for problem solving. (Neurofeedback is also training in self-regulation. It's simply biofeedback dedicated to the brain.)

Step number four is spirituality, which offers important concepts, work, and skills that will help lead you to inner peace. The philosophical ideas of Viktor Frankl provide inspiration for embracing life in a joyful, courageous, and loving way. You'll learn about the importance of having meaning in life as well as being resilient. You'll also see that those who experience nature as an aspect of their higher consciousness improve their ability to open up their channels. This book will introduce techniques for balancing your chakras and keeping your energy harmonious—other key factors to maintaining inner peace.

The last part is step five: heart. To find your loving heart and keep it open is most important in this step. Love and the poetry of Rumi are essential parts of this experience. Reading Rumi's poetry and understanding and loving yourself are the beginning of this journey. From self-love springs the love of all, including all of the beings in the universe. When your heart is open with love and compassion, you can then create your life through the positive choices you make. Love connects you to your inner peace.

Enjoy the Journey!

As you move through this journey, you will be asking the following:

- Who am I?
- Who sees when I see?
- Who hears when I hear?
- Who knows that I am aware?

Going through the steps—and gaining greater awareness of mind, body, brain, spirituality, and heart—will finally get you to your inner peace and your purpose.

Step 1: Mind

If you are depressed, you are living in the past.
If you are anxious, you are living in the future.
If you are at peace, you are living in the present.

—Lao Tzu

Jon's First Session

Jon walked into my office with a glum expression, and his shoulders slumped as he settled in a chair. Pulling a tissue from the box, he said, "I don't know what I'm going to do." Jon wiped his nose and started to cry. "I have problems sleeping," he told me. "I have migraine headaches and stomach problems. I have a beautiful wife and two great kids, and I'm miserable. The fire is out of me."

Jon grabbed another tissue and then continued. He said that he had just turned fifty and was experiencing a fear of dying. He mentioned that he was financially secure; his family had taken care of that. And there Jon sat, telling me that he could never say that he had done anything important for himself, for the world, or for anyone. He didn't know how good a father he was or how

1

his kids felt about him, how his wife felt about him, or how he felt about himself. He saw himself as a robot with no feelings and no passion—no anything. And then he asked me, "What can I do?"

"What do you want to do?" I asked him. "You mentioned that you were in therapy for five years, from when you were eighteen until twenty-three, and nothing changed. It sounds like you have been miserable for most of your life."

Jon nodded and then shook his head at the state of his life.

I told Jon that I wanted to help him with three areas: (1) understanding how he had created this reality for himself, by looking at his old patterns of thinking, believing, being, and behaving; (2) deciding who he was and what he wanted his life to be like; and (3) constructing the steps necessary to get himself to his goals.

Then I asked, "What did you hear me say, Jon, and what is your response to that?"

"Dr. Lita, I'm so depressed that I am willing to do almost anything," he answered. "However, I'm not interested in taking any kind of medication. But I'm tired of spending all these years complaining and blaming. I won't go on like this anymore."

"It sounds like you're willing to start the journey," I said. I then asked Jon to tell me about what growing up in his family was like.

"I'm the oldest of three children," he said, "and the only one that completed a college degree. My brother, Craig, is forty-eight, and he's still into sports and plays basketball with his buddies in Ohio. Craig is in his second marriage, but there are no children. My sister, Marianne, is four years younger than me, and she travels all over the world. She's not married and has no children, and we never know where she is."

Jon told me that his father was the CEO of a major insurance company. His dad had spent several years of his life in the fire service. He loved taking care of the land and people and teaching others how to protect nature. Jon continued, "Dad was very strict with all of us, including my mom, who was a nurse during my early childhood. We started out very poor, but my father had a great intellect as well as the drive and passion to get us to a point where we would be financially comfortable. He actually became very successful pretty quickly."

"Now tell me about you, Jon. What were you like as a child?" I prompted.

Jon shared that he was a creative kid. "I used to love to create, to make paintings, write, restore artwork, and invent things," he told me. "I loved surfing and learned it from my cousin at a very young age. As I got a little older, I spent a lot of time repairing classic cars."

Jon recalled that he frequently felt lonely as a child, because his mother was busy with his two younger siblings, and his dad was often away. "I was in my dream fantasy land a lot," he said, "and I felt a bit confused about the real world and growing up."

Jon's brother, Craig, got into sports at an early age, and his sister, Marianne, acted rebelliously, even as a little girl. Marianne got most of the attention in the family because she was always up to something and getting into trouble.

Jon and I were off to a good start. He was sharing good information that would be helpful in our work together.

Sharing these patterns of his life with me helped Jon become aware of what it was like for him living in his family. He was creative and also responsible in his family, being the eldest. Being the oldest made him behave as his father had—he was strict and conscientious in all that he did. Although he was creative, there was a lot of rigidity, and it was difficult for him to access that creative part because of his rigid thinking. As he went through this journey to get to that place of inner peace, Jon became aware that he needed to be more open, to have a loving heart, and to love himself. Through therapy and our work together, he became conscious and aware of the work that was necessary for him to do.

We will follow Jon's journey of personal growth throughout the book.

Making Sense of Your Reality

This journey requires you to look at the reality you have constructed for yourself. How do you go about building a reality? Well, your mind uses your five senses to take in the data you experience in the world. The information that comes in through your senses—taste, sight, sound, touch, and smell—is sorted in a way that confirms and validates the ongoing story being crafted. A person's vision of the world and the story that each individual believes to be his or her so-called reality is actually an internal product of the mind.

All the raw data you received during your growing-up years was constructed into a story. The mind establishes values along the way: *This is good. This is bad. This is to be feared. This produces pleasure.* Throughout your life, you assemble your values and your stories in an ongoing process.

I found Jon's description of his creativity as a child and his love for making, fixing, and remodeling things to be impressive. What had happened to the spirited, excited, creative energy of that young

Jon? Had the influence of a critical, demanding, strict, and rigid father impacted that beautiful energy?

Jon's ability to use analogy was also impressive. An analogy shows similarity between things that might seem different. If two things are alike in some ways, they are alike in some other ways as well. Analogy is used to help provide insight by comparing an unknown subject to one that is more familiar.

Jon mentioned many examples of his analogies over the course of our sessions. For example, Jon once said, "I just peeled off my coat," after his mother gave him a banana and asked, "Could you peel off the skin before I slice this into our cereal?"

The Voice inside Your Head

In case you haven't noticed, you have a mental dialogue going on inside your head that never stops. It keeps going on and on until you learn the skills to deal with it.

While you're driving away from home, you think, *Did I close the garage door and turn off the coffeepot? I didn't call my mother. Maybe I should stop and call her now. No, I don't want to call her right now.* Notice how the voice takes on both sides of the conversation. It doesn't care which side it takes as long as it gets to keep talking.

When you're ready for sleep at night, it's the voice inside your head that says, *What am I doing? I can't go to sleep yet. I forgot to call my mother. I remembered in the car this morning, but I didn't call. If I don't call now—oh, it's too late. I shouldn't call her now. I don't even know why I thought about it. I need to fall asleep. Oh boy, now I can't fall asleep. I'm not tired anymore. But I have a big day tomorrow, and I have to get up early.* No wonder you can't sleep. Why do you tolerate that voice talking to you all the time?

When you tune into it, this constant mental chatter will become obvious to you. It's actually a shocking realization when you first notice that your mind is continually talking. You might even try to yell at it in an attempt to shut it up. But then you realize that it is the voice yelling at the voice. It soon becomes obvious that you can't shut it up that way.

The best way to free yourself from this incessant chatter is to step back and view it objectively. View the voice as a vocalizing mechanism that is capable of making it appear as if someone is in there talking to you. Don't think about it; just notice it. In a way, the content of the voice's words doesn't matter, because it's just a voice talking inside your head.

An important step in true growth is realizing that you are not the voice of the mind—you are the one who hears it. Realize that none of these voices are who you are. Most of the talking is a waste of time and energy. If you spend your time hoping that it doesn't rain tomorrow, you're wasting your time. Your thoughts won't change the chance of rain. You will someday come to see that there is no use for that incessant internal chatter, and there is no reason to constantly attempt to figure everything out. Eventually, you will see that the real cause of problems is not life itself. It is the commotion the mind makes about life that causes the problems!

The mental voice talks for the same reason that a teakettle whistles. There is a buildup of energy inside that needs to be released. If you pay attention objectively, you will see that when there is a buildup of anxious, fearful, or desire-based energies inside, the voice becomes extremely active. For example, when you're angry with someone and feel like telling him or her off, watch yourself, and notice how many times the inner voice tells him or her off before you even see that person. When the energy builds inside, you want to do something about it. That voice talks because you're not okay inside, and talking is releasing the energy.

If you study this phenomenon carefully, you'll notice that the narration attempts to makes you feel more comfortable with the world around you. Like when you're a backseat driver, talking can make you feel as though things are more in your control. You feel as if you have some relationship with the things that are out of your control. By verbalizing mentally, you have brought that initial direct experience of the world into the realm of your thoughts. There, it becomes integrated with your other general thoughts, your analogies, and the thinking that makes up your value system and historical experience.

Look at the difference between your experience with the outside world and your interactions with the mental world. When you're just thinking, you are free to create whatever thoughts you want to in your mind, and your inner voice expresses these thoughts. You're accustomed to settling into the playground of the mind and creating and manipulating thoughts. This inner world is an alternate environment that is under your control. The outside world marches to its own rules.

When the inner voice narrates the outside world to you, those thoughts are side by side with all of your other thoughts, and they have equal weight with them. All of these thoughts intermix, which influences your experience of the world around you. You end up experiencing a personal presentation of the world, according to you, as opposed to a stark, unfiltered experience of what is really out there. This mental manipulation of the outer experience allows you to buffer reality as it comes in.

For example, there are many things that you see at a given moment, yet you narrate only a few of them. The ones you discuss in your mind are the ones that matter the most to you. As you are hearing all of those different ideas in your mind, you are controlling what your consciousness is experiencing and the idea of your present reality. The reality your mind constructs is not reality itself.

Pay attention to this, because we do it all the time. As you're walking outside on a chilly day, you start to shiver, and the voice says, *I feel cold.* Now, how did that help you? You already knew it was cold. You're the one experiencing the cold. Why is the voice telling you this information? Well, remember that you re-create the world within your mind because you can control your mind, whereas you cannot control the world. That's why you mentally talk about the cold weather.

So if you can't get the outside world the way you'd like it, you internally verbalize it, judge it, complain about it, and then decide what to do about it. This makes you feel more empowered. When your body experiences cold, there might be nothing you can do to control the temperature. But when your mind verbalizes, *It's cold*, you can tell yourself, "I'll be home in a few minutes and feel warm and cozy in the house."

In the thought world, there is always something you can do to control the experience. Basically, you re-create the outside world inside yourself, and then you live it in your mind. What if you decided not to do this? If you decided not to narrate the world and instead just consciously observed it, you would feel more open and exposed, because you wouldn't know what was going to happen next, and your mind is accustomed to helping you cope. It does this by processing your current experiences in a way that makes them fit within your view of the past and visions of the future. All of these mental processes help to create a semblance of control. If your mind didn't regulate your view of reality, you would become too uncomfortable. Reality is too real for most of us, so we temper it with the mind.

True personal growth is about transcending the part of you that is not okay and needs protection. You do this by constantly remembering that you are the one inside who notices the voice talking. The one inside who is aware that you are always talking to yourself about yourself is always silent. It is a doorway to the knowledge and the depths of your being. To be aware that you are listening to the voice talk is to stand on the threshold of a fantastic inner journey. If used properly, the same mental voice that has been a source of worry, distraction, and anxiety can become the launching ground for true spiritual awakening.

Later in this chapter, you'll have an opportunity to do exercises that will help you bring the mental voice under your control: journaling, self-talk, thought stopping, and self-love.

Back to Jon

During our first session, I shared this type of information with Jon. Near the end, I asked him, "What are you taking away from our session today?"

Jon said that he was on a new journey, and he felt committed to it. He would review his life growing up and pay attention to what it was like and how it felt. Jon said that he would keep a journal and write things down so that he could be clearer and understand how he thought and his process of creating his reality.

Jon realized that he was privileged, spoiled, and indulged as a kid growing up. He said he got everything he ever desired. Jon never had to get anything for himself or follow up on a task and complete it so that he could feel good about himself. Jon shared that he had never experienced a sense of confidence or a feeling of being happy from within. He told me that his family made fun of him because of his attempts to invent things, but he remembered that it was one of the hobbies that gave him the most joy.

"I'll work on my early stories and analogies and try to understand them and my old patterns so that I can see things with a new, clearer lens," Jon concluded.

Attachment Patterns

In working with his childhood stories, Jon took a look at his patterns. A pattern is a repeated way of doing something. A revealing pattern in how we think, feel, and behave as well as how we create our stories is our attachment style. These patterns are based on how we connected with our primary caregiver during childhood.

Attachment experiences in early childhood strongly influence whether an adult is secure in his or her relationships. For example, a secure child tends to believe that others will be there for him or her, because previous experiences have led the child to this conclusion. Once a child has developed such expectations, he or she tends to seek out relationship experiences that are consistent with those expectations. He or she will also perceive others in a way that is influenced by these beliefs.

Research has shown that our adult relationships are attachment relationships, and children who had secure relationships with parents will grow up to be secure in their romantic relationships. Having emotionally and physically available, attuned, responsive caregivers leads to the secure attachment style.

People with secure attachments have the following:

- long-term relationships
- high self-esteem
- support from their partners
- good sex

Individuals who had inconsistent parents who were sometimes there emotionally and physically and were sometimes not there will have anxious, resistant attachment patterns, characterized by the following:

- frequent breakups
- low self-esteem
- emotional instability
- lack of support
- jealousy

Other children found that their needs were usually not met by their parents, who were neglectful or even abusive physically or emotionally. They came to believe that communicating their needs was futile, as it would have no influence on the caregivers. This type of experience leads to a dismissive, avoidant pattern in adulthood. Individuals with this style will

- not put much effort into their relationships;
- find it easy to move from one relationship to another;

- prefer being alone;
- find excuses to avoid their partners, such as working long hours;
- not support their partners when required; and
- not disclose much about themselves.

These attachment styles create the thoughts that we have in our mind, the way we feel and behave, and our personality styles.

Secure Attachment

Personality style: Is balanced, has emotional equilibrium, is resilient, is able to make choices in life.

Thinking: "I am secure within myself. I can do what I need to do. I love myself."

Feeling: Relaxed, peaceful, positive, and joyful.

Behavior: Is emotionally and physically available to their relationships.

Anxious, Resistant Attachment

Personality style: Is passive-aggressive and narcissistic, has low self-esteem, experiences self-loathing.

Thinking style: "No one is ever there for me. People don't like to get as close as I like to be. I'm worried that my partner doesn't want to be with me."

Feeling: Unstable, emotionally dramatic, up and down emotionally.

Behavior: Is manipulative and not tuned into others' needs.

Dismissive, Avoidant Attachment

Personality style: Is paranoid and displays oppositional, obstructive patterns of thought and behavior.

Thinking style: "I am nothing. Others will harm me. People will destroy me."

Feeling: Anxious, nervous, fearful, and angry.

Behavior: Avoids people. Prefers being alone. Finds it difficult to trust and allow themselves to depend on others. Feels nervous when anyone gets too close. Does not share themselves.

You will be working with these attachment styles a little later in this chapter in the first exercise, journaling.

Twisted Thinking Patterns

In addition to any twisted thinking linked to your attachment style, there might be other distortions in the way you think. Below are ten of the most common mental distortions.

- **Blaming.** You don't take responsibility for the things you dislike in your life. Instead, you think about how other people are responsible and blame them for what you dislike.
- **All-or-nothing thinking.** You see things in black and white. If a situation falls short of perfect, you see it as a total failure. You cannot recognize a middle ground. For example, you went off your diet by having ice cream today, and you think, *I've blown it!*
- **Jumping to conclusions.** Without confirming or discussing something, you decide that you know what someone else is thinking or feeling—especially about you. For example, you don't hear from a friend, and you assume she doesn't like you anymore. In reality, the friend had a death in her family, and she has felt too sad to call.
- **Negative mental filter.** No matter what happens, you only see the negative. The positive is filtered out.
- **Overgeneralization.** You see one negative event, such as a rejection, as a never-ending pattern. The words *always* and *never* often enter your thinking. For example, your spouse doesn't return your call one day, and you think, *He never gives me the attention I need.*
- **Emotional reasoning.** Because you feel something, you assume that it must be true. For example, you worry that

your son won't get into his college of choice. You then assume that this must be what will happen.

- **"Should" statements.** You've created a list of "should" rules in your head. Now you believe you and everyone else has to follow them. This leads to guilt over your own actions and anger toward other offenders of your rules. These "should" statements are expectations of what you believe everyone must do because you say so.

- **Magnification.** You look at everything as being the worst. You always fear the worst. You create scenarios of disaster in your mind and become fearful, as if they really will happen. You mentally turn everything that might happen into a catastrophe.

- **Labeling.** Based on one incident, you globally label yourself or another person. There is no sense of putting things in perspective. For example, you forget where you put your parking ticket during a trip to the mall, and as a result, you tell yourself that you're stupid.

- **Victimhood.** You figure the cards are stacked against you and feel it's hopeless to try. You're always seeing yourself in the victim role. This leads to rigid thinking, behaving, and feeling, and you become stuck in this role of believing everything negative happens to you. You have to let go of that victim mentality in order to move forward.

Exercise 1: Journaling

It's time to work on an awareness of your mind and how you think. Have a notebook with you, and during the day, when you notice concern about what's happening in your outside world, write down what is going through your mind. This writing is to be free and uninhibited.

Also, take some time to write about what it was like growing up in your family. Write about some of the most significant events from your childhood and how you thought and felt about them. What were you like as a child?

Next, review what you wrote. While you're looking at your reflections, ask yourself the following questions:

a. **What patterns do you see in the stories from your early memories of what it was like growing up?** (A pattern is a standard way of thinking, feeling, and behaving that is repeated.) For instance, from reviewing his stories, Jon discovered his rigidness and all-or-nothing thinking. He also saw that he had been an anxious child and put himself in the anxious, resistant attachment-style category. (See the discussion of patterns in the last two sections.)

Your stories will remind you of what your way of thinking was, and eventually, you will construct new ways of thinking and new stories that are more appropriate for the changes you are making. Jon became more conscious of his thoughts that were paralyzing him. He said, "I used to be so afraid. Because of my rigid way of thinking, I was unable to let go of the anxious thoughts that prohibited me from moving forward. Now I'm able to release those feelings, thoughts, and behaviors. Also, I have a new understanding and vocabulary, like 'I can do it,' 'I will do it,' and 'It's time that I jumped in and checked it out, and then I will know if it is for me or if it is not for me.' Instead of using fear, I'm now using the experience of the situation to tell and guide me as to what's the best for me."

b. **What are the voices saying, and how are their words impacting you?** In Jon's case, his voices were initially paranoid, telling him of the fearful possibilities of all choices he might make, based in anxiety and trepidation. That was what kept him paralyzed all his life from doing things. Later, he became more open-minded about trying new things and allowing the situation to guide him. He became successful at jumping in and then appraising the situation. He let go and accepted that there would be mistakes made, but he understood that "In the Art of living, any mistake is a new creation." He liked that idea and began to notice how much he had learned and grown from listening to his new stories and his new voice.

c. **What is the emotional impact on your body from thinking about your stories and experiences from your early life?** Jon talked about his childhood as would someone with post-traumatic stress disorder (PTSD), in which the person relives the traumas his or her body experienced earlier. For example, every time Jon thought about being punished as a child, his body got tense, he clenched his jaw, and he felt stressed.

Over time, you want to construct a new story for what you have going on in your mind. This is the journey to creating your best life. It is done with the steps in this book and the recognition and understanding of your patterns of thinking, behaving, and feeling. Keep journaling as you are reading and working with the book, and notice how you and your stories are changing. Write about the changes.

The Self-Healing Personality

The humanistic psychologist Abraham Maslow spent a good part of his influential career focused on the positive, growth-oriented aspects of human beings. He considered what made them well and kept them healthy. Dr. Maslow recognized that healthy people need to achieve balance in their basic biological needs, and then they need to obtain affection and self-respect.

The biological needs—physical fitness, nutrition, good sleep patterns, a healthy body, and a healthy mind—were the basic foundation of his hierarchy to achieve self-actualization. When you are self-actualized, you are operating at your highest level— you are all that you can be.

We learned a lot from Dr. Maslow. I now believe that the most important questions in modern health care should not focus on artificial hearts and cancer chemotherapy but on the following questions: "Who stays well?" and "What is a self-healing personality?"

The self-actualized person has a self-healing personality. Some aspects of people with self-healing personalities are as follows:

1. They make up their optimistic minds to be healthy.
2. They have a sense of control and choice in their lives.
3. They have a commitment to higher goals and principles.
4. They are resilient.
5. They have an ability to integrate socially.

6. They live in environments of challenge and excitement.
7. They have a sense of creative self-fulfillment, which produces the will to thrive and the positive emotions that are at the core of good health.

Let's look at what it means to be resilient. Resiliency is the capacity to adapt successfully in the presence of risk and adversity. This adaptation happens with optimistic thinking. There is a level of fitness on a thinking level.

When we adjust our thinking in this positive way, we learn to adapt and overcome situations. We don't just see the problems; we see situations that we have to evaluate, understand, and resolve.

This way of being helps us adjust to difficult and challenging life experiences. We learn to confront and handle stressful life events.

These experiences, in turn, help us grow and thrive. We bounce back so that we can beat the odds. We learn how to negotiate adversity.

Another essential element of self-healing personalities is emotional equilibrium, or keeping yourself in balance on an emotional level. When a degree of emotional equilibrium and balance is maintained, the body's physiological processes can work most efficiently to keep your cells and organs functioning at their best. The challenge is to maintain this emotional equilibrium, a complex process that depends on the individual's resources and his or her environmental demands. Your resiliency plays a major role.

Optimists vs. Pessimists

Optimism is an overall expectation for desirable future outcomes. You can be optimistic and goal directed while not taking on more than you can handle. You can maintain a hopeful attitude and have a future orientation. By "future orientation," I mean imagining good outcomes and engaging in positive future life planning. In your daily life, you can choose to pursue optimism instead of pessimism.

In contrast, pessimists tend to think, *It's all my fault. I mess up everything, I hate myself, and disappointment is the story of my life.* Pessimists are more likely to mentally check out and put their heads in the sand.

Realistic optimists have a habitual way of exploring events. They see the negative but do not dwell on it or overgeneralize about the positive. They have the ability to size up a situation dispassionately while still staying open to future possibilities and new ideas and experiences.

> The pessimist complains about the wind;
> The optimist expects it to change:
> The realistic optimist adjusts the sails.
> —William Arthur Ward

Optimists, as compared to pessimists, have better individual well-being. According to Martin Seligman, author of *Learned Optimism*, these individuals use more-effective coping strategies and are positive, productive, and energized. They are better liked and supported. They also make higher salaries.

Rather than clinging to the past, optimists use previous experiences as teaching lessons for the future. They believe that the future is not something that just happens, but something they can help create.

Here is how an optimist thinks about him- or herself: *I have confidence in my ability to bring about positive outcomes and have a sense of personal control. That is, I hold the belief that things can change for the better and that I have the ability to bring about such changes. I focus on my abilities and will never lose sight of the strengths and virtues that reside within me.*

More Techniques to Support Your Awakening

In addition to journaling, other techniques in this chapter will assist you in becoming awake to your processes. When you are awake, the "lights are on." In a state of awareness, you can clearly use your mind to choose the way you make choices in your life.

Mindful breathing will help you calm yourself down. With self-talk and thought stopping, you will start talking to yourself in positive ways to change your narrative and stop the old, negative tape that is relentless. Let's start with the breathing technique.

Breath is the bridge,
which connects life to consciousness,
which unites your body to your thoughts.
—Thich Nhat Hanh

Mindful breathing allows you to stop and become mindful of you—what you're thinking, how you're behaving, what choices you have, and what you should do. Let's go back to another session I had with Jon.

"How can I be calm when I know all the negative things that I'm thinking all the time about my life and me?" asked Jon. "My mind races a million miles an hour. My heart is also racing. I feel sweaty. Being alone and my fear remind me of when I was a little boy and had no one to protect me. That made me feel anger."

"Okay, Jon, we'll deal with those issues later in our session," I told him. "For now, I want to introduce you to a behavior that will help you learn to self-regulate your calmness—something you've never learned in your life. You'll learn how to allow feelings to arise and how to express them in a way that you're comfortable with. For now, I want you to realize that there's nothing you can do about the situation, only how you deal with it. The work is to go within for now. Focusing your awareness on your breathing is an excellent way to settle your mind and to learn to relax." I paused for a moment while Jon got a glass of water from the dispenser.

"Our breathing often mirrors our emotions," I explained to Jon after he was seated again. "For example, we gasp with amazement, choke with sadness, or sigh with relief. Breathing becomes irregular and ragged with anger, and it stops with fear. That's why your last panic attack brought you into emergency care—because you were holding your breath."

I was making Jon aware that breathing is involved in everything we do. Correct breathing is essential to a healthy life. The purpose of breathing is to get oxygen from the air into your body and to blow off waste products, such as carbon dioxide. Slight changes in oxygen content in the brain can alter the way you feel and behave.

When you get angry or stressed out, your breathing pattern changes immediately. Breathing becomes shallower, and the rate increases significantly. This breathing pattern is inefficient, and the oxygen content in an angry person's blood is lowered. There is less oxygen available to your brain, and you might become more irritable, impulsive, and confused, which can cause you to make bad decisions.

Changing your breathing can shift your attention and your mood. Breathing patterns will both reflect and redirect your emotions. Becoming more mindful of the link between your breathing and your emotional state will help you feel more empowered and more in control.

Exercise 2: Mindful Breathing, Part I

You can learn mindful breathing quickly, as you will see by doing the following:

1. Make a tight fist hard enough to cause mild pain.
2. Observe what happens to your breathing. Does your breathing stop or become shallow?
3. Relax for a moment, and then make another tight fist, but continue to breathe slowly and deeply.
4. Observe what happens to the tension in your fist and your sensation of pain. With slow, deep breathing, the tension and pain should be reduced.

When I gave Jon the exercise above, I explained, "It is difficult to maintain tension, anger, pain, fear, or anxiety while breathing in a relaxed way. Pay attention to your breathing the next time you start noticing upsetting thoughts. Awareness and mindful breathing are powerful ways to gain control over stress and emotions."

Studies have shown that hyperventilation, or overbreathing, is a prime suspect in anxiety, and it can leave you feeling light-headed, anxious, and depressed. The main difficulty is not breathing too quickly; it is breathing with the upper part of the chest instead of the abdomen (i.e., belly). We all start out in life by breathing from our bellies—our belly rises with each breath in and falls with each breath out. Watch children's bellies as they breathe. You'll see that their bellies are involved. As adults, many of us replace belly breathing with chest breathing—a shallow, rapid breathing pattern associated with tension and anxiety.

Exercise 3: Mindful Breathing, Part II

Lie down on your back on a couch or bed, and close your eyes. Place one hand gently on your chest and the other hand on your abdomen. Without changing your normal breathing pattern, observe your body as you inhale normally. Which hand rises the most—the one on your chest or the one on your belly? Most of my clients tell me their hands on their chests rose more. This is because they're breathing with their chests and not their abdomens.

Continue lying down on the couch or bed. You might wish to bend your knees, keeping your knees and feet slightly apart. Loosen your belt and any restrictive clothing. Place your hands gently below your belly button. Close your eyes, and imagine a balloon inside your abdomen. Each time you breathe in, imagine the balloon filling with air. Your hands will gently rise. Each time you breathe out, imagine the balloon deflating. Your hands will gently settle lower down. Focus on the sound and the sensation of your breathing, and you will become more relaxed. At first, belly breathing might feel unusual, but with practice, it becomes second nature, and you will discover its relaxing benefits.

Many clients ask me how they will be able to respond to issues with high energy if they become so calm and relaxed. I tell them that when you're in this state of being calm and relaxed, all of your senses—mind, body, soul, and spirit—are primed and at your command. It's empowering and powerful. There will be no tension or anxiety to take away your energy or interfere with your ability to function mindfully and quickly.

My clients often notice that while they focus on their breathing, they are in the moment. They don't hear or think about their inner voices at all. If you start to hear those thoughts while practicing mindful breathing, change your breathing response to a more relaxed one. The transition will automatically calm you down and decrease any stress you might have, because you are present in the moment when you're breathing mindfully, and breathing is all you are focusing on.

It might be a good idea to create a "breathing room" in your home. It is interesting that we have eating rooms, guest rooms, television rooms, computer rooms, bedrooms, and bathrooms—everything except a room for cultivating inner peace. Wouldn't it be great if you could create a place in your home as a breathing room, a peaceful sanctuary? It could become part of your daily life, not just a place of refuge during an emotional storm.

Each morning before leaving home, you could spend some time, perhaps a half hour, in this space of inner peace and practice mindful breathing. Make it a habit. Walk quietly into the room, sound your favorite bell (you could use Tibetan tingsha bells), and come back to yourself through mindful breathing. With this practice, the day will always begin well. In the evening, before going to sleep, you can also visit this special room, sound the bell, and breathe mindfully. Again, I suggest spending one half hour. This practice will help you to end your night and begin your next day peacefully. Practicing mindful breathing starts the process of awakening.

Revisiting the Voice

Earlier in the chapter, I wrote about self-talk—the internal voices inside our heads, the running commentary about everything we do. This internal monologue can be negative and self-limiting or positive and growth producing. Becoming aware of this internal chatter is the first step in taking charge of this voice.

These internal monologues are present in everyone. They have been formed by your parents, teachers, religious teachers (or other authority figures), and reactions to certain events. By the time you are an adult, they have been incorporated into your personality. You don't need those people to tell you what to do anymore (they are living inside your head!).

You'll notice that your inner dialogues reflect the patterns of your thinking, being, and behaving, and they become projected onto all your relationships as well as how you think, feel, and behave in your life now.

Thoughts precede moods, so if you think unhappy thoughts, you feel unhappy. Self-talk results from your thoughts making themselves known to you. Hearing somebody else talking negatively is bad enough, so imagine how much more potent your own inner voice is. If you tell yourself you're a failure, guess what—you will be! If you tell yourself that you can succeed, then you have a better chance of succeeding.

When self-talk is negative, you will perceive things as more stressful. If you're telling yourself that you are dealing with a difficult and unfair situation, then it becomes more stressful to deal with. But if you reframe your words and think, *This is a challenge* or *This is a test*—using self-talk that is optimistic rather than pessimistic—you will likely have positive effects emotionally, mentally, spiritually, and physically. Research has proven this.

When you tell yourself that you can't handle something (or have some other self-limiting thought), you tend to stop looking for solutions. In contrast, saying, "How can I handle this?" or "What can I do?" will help you feel more hopeful and produce creative solutions.

Exercise 4: Self-Talk

In order to deal with negative self-talk, you must first become aware of your inner dialogue and notice when it shows up and what it is telling you. You have to be vigilant and pay attention to the process with your observing ego. The fact that you realize the voice is not yours and that you can discuss it and be aware of it in your meditation means that it is something that you do and not what you are. You must now pay attention to what you think. By paying attention to what you think, you can begin to observe your inner voice without buying into what your mind is telling you. You are now able to catch the repetitive nature of your thoughts.

When you're able to do this, you'll realize that you don't have to react to the thoughts presented by your mind. Reacting is a habit, and by being aware, noticing, and catching on to that inner voice, your observing ego will become your adviser. That awareness will allow you to notice the thoughts and choose to do what you have always done or choose to do something different.

Stopping these negative thoughts and self-limiting ideas and creating a positive internal dialogue will reduce your stress. Know that your self-talk, what you say to yourself, is important and influences your self-esteem and confidence. Talking encouragingly to yourself will empower you. The next section teaches you thought stopping, which will help you do further work with your internal chatter.

Yes, You Can Stop Your Thoughts

Thought stopping is the ability to stop focusing on a thought that is bothersome to you. We cannot get rid of a thought without replacing it with another. Therefore, when using this technique, you substitute a healthy thought for an unhealthy thought. This practice will help you break the power of cues that led you to unhealthy patterns or habits.

Before you can practice thought stopping, you must learn mindful breathing and relaxation. It is important to practice mindful breathing so that when you tell yourself to stop, you'll be in a calmer state, which will enable you to replace your negative thought with a healthy, rational image and thought.

Exercise 5: Thought Stopping

Now use this technique to eliminate an undesired thought that you have. This will help you change the story you're telling yourself. You'll be working with one of your own thoughts that is affecting the way you're feeling and behaving. Look for a thought that is producing emotional pain.

1. Take a deep breath, close your eyes, and select the thought you want to stop. For example, you might be thinking, *They're going to fire me!* (This thought falls into the jumping-to-conclusions thinking pattern.)
2. Think of the situation that the thought is related to in your life now. For example, perhaps there are cutbacks at your company.
3. Now visualize and meditate on all the positive things you have learned from this situation—whatever you can identify, no matter how big or small. For example, you learned of training that will enable you to apply for better positions in the company. You signed up and are now involved in that training.
4. Feel the positive emotions associated with getting benefit from your situation. For example, you could enjoy the feelings associated with taking action about the problem.
5. Now formulate a summary thought that you can think instead of the negative interpretation. For example, *I am taking the steps necessary to take care of myself.*

Jon used this technique for a situation at work. His difficult boss criticized him all the time for not cleaning off his desk when he left for the day. The boss would remark, "Is it fun living in a pigsty?" At first, Jon told himself, *I'm a slob. My desk is a pigsty.* However, he realized that his desk was actually not messy or disorganized. He just liked to keep his current work folders handy.

With a little work, Jon learned to say to himself, *I'm okay. My desk is the way I want it. Stop saying I'm a slob.* He would repeat saying "stop" in his head. Jon said that this practice helped him feel calm. Jon was visualizing that he was okay, and with time, his boss's comments no longer bothered him. Jon couldn't change the situation, but he changed himself and how he was reacting to it.

Learning to Love and Be Compassionate to Yourself

Some of the thoughts you tap into in your mind might be negative and colored with self-loathing. This is not unusual. Therefore, it's important, before ending this chapter, to consider the opposite perspective on one's self.

Self-love and compassion rise from the selfless virtues of tolerance, forgiveness, sympathetic understanding, and empathy. Self-love and compassion go hand in hand with wisdom, as if they were the two wings of a bird.

Many of us have been taught to hate ourselves, to consider ourselves inferior, to think our needs are not important. That is why we sabotage ourselves. When you have been neglected and told you are not worthy of loving or compassionate treatment, self-hate can affect every action you take and every aspect of yourself. Some readers might have experienced verbal, spiritual, emotional, physical, or sexual abuse, and these individuals might have been told they were worthless, trash, someone to be hated.

In essence, self-love is being free to be oneself. Self-love should not be confused with narcissism and egocentricity. It comes from a process of healthy personal growth in which the actualization of your personal potentials—especially in the service of others—brings you joy and happiness and enhances your self-worth rather than your conceit.

To love ourselves is to be continuously in touch with this source of joy and happiness and to learn to appreciate the goodness we have in us. All egoistic and narcissistic tendencies, including self-aggrandizement and self-abasement, erode self-love. Our willingness to open our hearts and minds to accept all situations and all people, touch our pain and sorrow with tenderness, and reach out to others in need of help is a power so warm that it heals us, so strong that it overcomes, and so radiant that it illuminates. Out of self-love, the power of love and compassion grows.

Exercise 6: Self-Love

This exercise will help you focus inward and see if you have self-love. Set a timer for five minutes, start the clock, and then begin talking about all the positive things you can think of about yourself. If possible, record what you're saying so that you can listen to it from time to time. It's helpful to also jot down the points to increase your self-awareness. If it's not possible to say this out loud, then write down who you are as a list. But remember to include only positive statements.

Your statements may include comments like the following:

- "I'm a fun person to be with."
- "I make great pancakes."

- "I love music and dancing."
- "I know I have a lot to learn, and I'm working on that in my life."

Many of my patients with low self-esteem have tremendous difficulty with this exercise. After one minute, they'll say, "Am I through yet?"

I tell them, "When you start and I can't stop you from enjoying and telling me about all the wonder that you are, then you have graduated from this therapy." So be patient with yourself if it takes you awhile to be able to do this activity for five minutes. Start where you are, even if it's only coming up with one or two positive things, and work up to five minutes.

Self-love is gentle and accepting. It is kind, compassionate, and forgiving. When you can achieve self-love and self-compassion, then you can live your life with others in that same way. It's imperative that you first learn to love yourself.

When you have decided to love yourself, a feeling will emerge from deep within. You will learn how to receive love and compassion from others. You will love and respect the person you are.

Repeat positive, caring, compassionate messages to yourself over and over. Offer comfort and love to the little kid inside who was hurt, neglected, and abused. Be loving and compassionate with yourself; surround yourself with loving, compassionate people; and you'll be on your way!

There is more to explore on the topic of love in the section "Step 5: Heart."

* * * * *

So what do you want the new story of your life to be like? Can you recognize any special passion that you have? Jon's love of creativity with inventing new things by using old parts is an example of this. If a thought excites you, keeping your mind and heart open can be an important part of finding a new story that includes passion and purpose.

Later, Jon told me, "I can see my old self through the eyes of my new self." Jon noticed that he was letting go of the old stories he had held on to that had kept him paralyzed in a negative way and unable to be free to see the wonder of himself. Finally, he was working with new ideas that were clear, clean, and without the emotional baggage of yesterdays.

Step 2: Body

You can't stop the waves, but
you can learn to surf.
—Jon Kabat-Zinn

How many times have you said or heard someone say something like "Relax," "Calm down," or "Chill out"? If you're on the receiving end of such a comment, following the person's advice might not be so easy. Relaxation is a skill, and it's an important one to learn to reduce the impacts of stress on your body.

Stress and the Relaxation Response

Austrian Canadian endocrinologist Hans Selye did groundbreaking research in the 1950s on stress. He found that the human reaction to stress is an adaptive biological response with impacts on the entire system. Mental attention to an approaching threat triggers an alarm and a mobilization response, preparing the body for emergency action. The stress response activates the limbic, or emotional, brain and the hypothalamus, which then stimulates a large portion of the sympathetic nervous system and the endocrine system. The result is a flood of stress hormones (including ACTH), elevated blood sugar, and hyperarousal of many internal organs and functions. The individual will notice elevated heart rate, tense muscles, rapid breathing, and a variety of intense emotional states. This adaptive response prepares the individual to flee or fight the threat. In ideal circumstances, the threat passes and the individual can return to a more relaxed psychophysiological state.

In 1975, American physician Herbert Benson established that just as there is a human stress response, with negative effects on the body, there is also a relaxation response, with a healing or restorative impact on the human physiology and mind. Benson began by investigating transcendental meditation and its effects on physiology. The effects were the exact opposite of the stress response: a reduction in stress-hormone levels, lowered heart rate and blood pressure, relaxed muscles, and emotional calm. Benson reviewed the literature on Eastern meditation, Christian mysticism, and relaxation practices, and he found that most approaches shared a common formula with three elements:

1. a quiet environment,
2. cultivation of a passive mental attitude (letting go), and
3. the use of a mental device to focus attention.

Benson hypothesized that this relaxation response appears to underlie the beneficial effects of many schools of Eastern and Western meditation, yoga, and relaxation skills training.

Benson's research showed the clinical benefits of cultivating the relaxation response in lowered blood pressure, reduced anxiety, smoke cessation, and reduced drug and alcohol dependence.

Time to Chill Out

There are many paths to learning relaxation skills. I've included some relaxation exercises in this chapter that have been clinically studied and proven to be effective. The first is progressive muscle relaxation, which basically involves the tensing and relaxing of the various muscle groups while engaging in deep belly breathing.

I recommend that you read the following exercise into an audio recorder and play it back when you wish to do the exercise.

Exercise 1: Progressive Relaxation

Please do this progressive-relaxation exercise twice a day—in the morning before you get out of bed and at night before you go to sleep. Tense and relax all the muscles of your body to achieve body awareness.

Continue deep breathing throughout this entire exercise.

Relaxation of Arms
(Time: 4–5 minutes)

Settle back as comfortably as you can as you lie in bed. Let yourself relax to the best of your ability. As you relax, clench your right fist. Clench your fist tighter and tighter, and study the tension as you do so. Keep it clenched, and feel the tension in your right fist, hand, and forearm. Now relax, let the fingers of your right hand become loose, and observe the contrast in your feelings. Next, let yourself go, and become more relaxed all over. Once more, clench your right fist tightly, hold it, and notice the tension again. Now let go, relax your fingers, straighten them out, and notice the difference once more. Now repeat that process with your left fist. Clench your left fist while the rest of your body relaxes; clench the left fist, making your hand tight and tense. Now do the opposite of tension: relax, and feel the difference. Continue relaxing for a while. Now clench both fists tighter and tighter; make both fists tense, the forearms tense. Study the sensations—and then relax. Straighten out your fingers, and feel that relaxation. Continue relaxing for a while. Now clench your fists tighter and tighter; make your fists and forearms tense. Study the sensations—and relax. Straighten out your fingers, and feel the relaxation. Continue relaxing your hands and forearms.

Now bend your elbows, and tense your biceps (the muscles at the front of the upper arms). Tense them harder, and study the feelings of tension. Now straighten out your arms and let them relax, and feel the difference once again. Let the relaxation develop. Now, once more, tense your biceps, holding the tension and observing it carefully. Next, straighten your arms, and relax to the best of your ability. Each time, pay close attention to your feelings when you tense up and when you relax. Now straighten your arms—straighten them so that you feel most of the tension in the triceps (the muscles along the backs of your arms). Stretch your arms, and feel that tension. Now relax. Get your arms back into a comfortable position. Allow the relaxation to proceed on its own. Your arms should feel comfortably heavy as you allow them to relax. Straighten your arms once again so that you feel the tension in the triceps. Feel that tension—and now relax. Concentrate on pure relaxation in your arms without any tension. Get your arms comfortable, and allow them to relax further and further. Continue relaxing your arms ever further. Even when your arms seem fully relaxed, try to go a bit further. Try to achieve deeper and deeper levels of relaxation.

Facial Area with Neck, Shoulders, and Upper Back
(Time: 4–5 minutes)

Let all your muscles go loose and heavy. Just settle back quietly and comfortably. Next, wrinkle up your forehead. Wrinkle it tighter—and now stop wrinkling your forehead. Relax, and smooth it out. Picture your entire forehead and scalp becoming smoother as the relaxation increases. Now frown, and crease your brows. Study the tension. Next, let go of the tension, and once again, smooth out your forehead. Now close your eyes tighter and tighter. Feel the tension in the eye muscles, and now relax your eyes. Close your eyes gently and comfortably, and notice the relaxation. Now clench your jaws by biting your teeth together gently, and study the tension throughout your jaws. Now relax, and let your lips part slightly. Appreciate the relaxation. Now press your tongue hard against the roof of your mouth. Look for the tension, and now let your tongue return to the comfortable and relaxed position—notice the difference. Now press your lips together tighter and tighter so that you feel tension in the lip muscles—and now relax the lips. Notice the contrast between tension and relaxation. Feel the relaxation all over your face—all over your forehead and scalp, eyes, jaws, lips, tongue, and throat. Let the relaxation progress further and further. Now attend to your neck muscles. Gently press your head back as far as it can go, and feel the tension in the neck; slowly and gently, roll it to the right and feel the tension shift. Now roll it to the left. Straighten your head, and bring it forward, pressing your chin against your chest. Let your head return to a comfortable position, and study the relaxation. Allow the relaxation to develop. Shrug your shoulders up to both sides of your head, and feel the tension in the trapezius muscles. Now drop your shoulders and relax, and feel the relaxation. Once again, shrug your shoulders, and move them around and rotate them. Bring them up and forward and back, and feel the tension in your shoulders and in your upper back. Now drop your shoulders once more, and relax. Let the relaxation spread deep into the shoulders, right into your back muscles; relax your neck, throat, jaws, and other facial areas as the pure relaxation takes over and grows ever deeper.

Chest, Stomach, and Lower Back
(Time: 4–5 minutes)

Relax your entire body to the best of your ability. Feel that comfortable heaviness that accompanies relaxation. Breathe easily and freely, in and out. Notice how the relaxation increases as you exhale. Just feel that relaxation. Now breathe in, and fill your lungs; inhale deeply, and hold your breath. Study the tension, and then exhale. Let the walls of your chest grow loose, and push the air out automatically. Continue relaxing and breathing freely and gently. Feel the relaxation, and enjoy it. With the rest of your body as relaxed as possible, fill your lungs again with your belly breath, holding the breath deeply, and then breathe out and appreciate the relief. Next, breathe normally. Continue relaxing your chest, and let the relaxation spread to your back, shoulders, neck, and arms. Merely let go and enjoy the relaxation.

Now direct your attention to your lower back. Arch up your back, making your lower back hollow, and feel the tensions as you do so. Try to keep the rest of your body as relaxed as possible. Try to localize the tension throughout your lower-back area. Now relax your lower and upper back, spreading the relaxation to your stomach, chest, and shoulders, ever farther and deeper.

Hips, Thighs, and Calves, Followed
by Complete Body Relaxation
(Time: 4–5 minutes)

Let go of all tensions, and relax. Now flex your buttocks and your thighs by pressing down your heels as hard as you can. Relax, and note the difference. Now straighten your knees; flex your thigh muscles again, holding the tension; and then relax your hips and your thighs. Allow the relaxation to proceed on its own. Press your toes downward away from your face so that your calf muscles become tense. Study that tension, and then relax your feet and your calves. This time, bend your toes toward your face so that you feel tension along your shins (the fronts of the lower legs). Bring those toes up—and now relax again. Keep relaxing for a while; allow yourself to relax further all over. Relax your feet, ankles, calves, shins, knees, thighs, buttocks, and hips. Feel the heaviness in your lower body as you relax still further. Now spread the relaxation to your stomach, waist, and lower back. Let go more and more deeply. Make sure that no tension has crept into your throat; relax your neck, your jaws, and all of your facial muscles. Keep relaxing your whole body for a while. Allow yourself to relax.

Now you can become twice as relaxed as you are merely by taking in a deep breath and slowly exhaling. Keeping your eyes closed, take in a deep breath, and feel yourself becoming heavier. Then let it out slowly, and feel how heavy and relaxed you have become.

In a state of perfect relaxation, you'll feel unwilling to move a single muscle in your body. Think about the effort that would be required to raise your right arm, and as you think about the effort that would be required to raise your right arm, see if you can notice any tensions that might have crept into your shoulder and your arm. Now decide not to lift the arm but to continue relaxing. Observe the relief and the disappearance of the tension. Carry on relaxing like that, and when you are ready and wish to get up, count backward from four to one. You'll feel fine, refreshed, wide awake, and calm.

The Power of Creative Visualization

The second type of skill that I'm presenting in step two is the use of creative visualization. A book written by personal-development pioneer Shakti Gawain popularized this technique. It is a process of using your imagination to create what you want in your life. You're already using this technique every day—every minute, in fact. It's your natural power of imagination—the basic creative energy of the universe—which you use constantly, whether or not you're aware of it. You need to become conscious of this process and learn how to use your imagination in positive ways.

Imagination is the ability to create an idea, a mental picture, or a feeling or sensation of something. In creative visualization, you use your imagination to create a clear image, idea, or feeling of something you wish to manifest. Then you continue to focus on the idea, feeling, or picture regularly, giving it positive energy until it becomes objective reality—in other words, until you actually achieve what you have been imagining.

You cannot use this technique to control people or anything like that. It's simply a process in which you image and create what you want. For instance, one of my psychology students told me that she imagined that she would like to have twenty patients a week when she went into private practice. She creatively visualized that experience. Years later, she told me that her patient rate was staying at twenty. If she lost two clients, she would get a phone call with two new referrals!

To use creative visualization, it is not necessary to believe in any metaphysical or spiritual ideas, though you must be willing to entertain certain concepts as being possible. The only thing necessary is the desire to enrich your knowledge and experience, along with an open-enough mind to try something new in a positive spirit.

This technique works best if you completely relax and then use your imagination to create an image of what you want.

I recommend that you read the following exercise into an audio recorder and play it back when you wish to do the exercise.

Exercise 2: Going to Your Perfect Place of Relaxation

Lie down in a comfortable position. Relax. Close your eyes. Take a deep breath, and relax some more. Make a mental note to concentrate on deep breathing throughout this entire exercise.

Let go of all the tension in your body. Feel your eyelids relaxing. Allow this relaxation to flow pleasantly down through all the parts of your body. Now say each of the following sentences out loud:

My arms and legs are heavy and warm.

My heartbeat is calm and regular.

My body breathes itself.

My abdomen is warm.

My forehead is cool.

My mind is quiet and still.

I am at peace.

Now create your perfect place of relaxation—it could be sitting on the beach, walking in the woods, floating in a pool, or hugging the trees in your garden. Create the scene using all of your senses. For instance, if your place of relaxation is the beach, you can taste the salt water on your lips, hear the sea gulls, and feel the warm sun on your body. Once you're there, explore and enjoy your special place for several minutes. Then open your eyes, and give yourself a minute before moving on with your day.

Biofeedback: A Tool for Learning Self-Regulation Skills

Biofeedback is a process through which you can learn how to use feedback from electronic monitoring of your body's responses. I started working with it in a clinical setting during the 1970s. The goal is to train individuals how to acquire voluntary control of their bodies' reactions. Let's say that a patient is clenching his or her fists when stressed. By being hooked up to the biofeedback machine, he or she will become aware of the tension in his or her fists through a sound from the machine, the readout, display screens, etc. Over time, he or she will learn to be more aware of this reaction to stress when off the machine and, thus, will be empowered to choose a different, more soothing response. Training includes practice in using empowering techniques, such as deep breathing.

The effect of biofeedback training is similar to the effect of training wheels on a bicycle. Once you learn to balance your body, you no longer need the training wheels. The body does not forget.

Initially, I was involved in doctoral research using this adjunct treatment for psychosomatic and stress-related disorders, along with psychotherapy. We had many interesting and provocative studies during this period, including working with anxiety, depression, sleep disorders, headaches, breathing issues, pain, and fatigue, to mention a few.

The use of biofeedback is one of the most compelling examples of a way to support the body's ability to learn to self-regulate and bring itself back into balance. It offers individuals an opportunity to participate in their own healing process and is an adventure in self-regulation. If you need support to learn to reduce stress, biofeedback is an excellent option. Biofeedback sessions are offered by psychotherapists, trained clinicians, and other health professionals.

At my Biofeedback and Neurofeedback Treatment Center, we use the biofeedback equipment to assess the issues to work on as well as how a patient is progressing with self-regulation. On the patient's first visit, he or she will receive an initial comprehensive evaluation. If necessary, a schedule of biofeedback training sessions will be established for them.

During a session, noninvasive sensors are placed on specific sites on the body. The sensors enable the body's responses to be displayed on computer screens by using a full range of specially designed display screens that simulate arcade games and tell stories with animated, colorful designs. Muscle tension, temperature, heart rate, respiration, and skin conductance can all be measured. Audio and visual reinforcement is produced, immediately assisting the patient in replacing unwanted chronic patterns and symptoms with more-adaptive responses that help bring the body back into balance.

The treatment model we use at my center is based on a biopsychosocial-spiritual approach. Cognitive-behavioral therapeutic techniques are integrated into the work by a psychotherapist, which helps the client understand his or her behavior and teaches new behaviors, new options, and how to gain control of his or her life, as the person will see that he or she has choices.

Using biofeedback instrumentation as a tool, a client is be able to "see" and "hear" the progress of the mind-body-soul-spirit bridge. The client will feel accepted and supported in his or her healing process. Jon said he felt relaxed and calm during his biofeedback sessions. One day, when he was hooked up to the biofeedback machine, the EMG (or electromyography, which measures muscle activity) muscle reading showed high numbers, meaning that he was stressed, and the temperature showing the blood flow indicated a low reading, meaning he was constricting his blood flow. This was a sign of stress that Jon had not been aware of. He mentioned that he had seen a bad accident on the freeway while driving to the office and that it had produced this experience for him. After we talked about it, he became mindful that these were ways he responded to stress. Self-calming actions that we worked with included taking a deep breath, relaxing his shoulders, and keeping calm thoughts in his mind.

Biofeedback equipment can be costly, but with changes in mobile technology, some biofeedback tools have become much more affordable and accessible. Although they do not replace biofeedback training with an experienced therapist or other clinician with this skill set, these home-use devices and apps can be great ways of monitoring the benefits of the helpful responses you learned from your therapist. There are many apps out there, emphasizing different aspects of the possible biofeedback assessments.

The Origins of Biofeedback

The concept of biofeedback was introduced at a conference in Santa Monica, California, in 1969. The image of electronic equipment guiding human beings to a greater awareness and control over their own physiology and consciousness appealed to both white-coated experimental scientists and the white-robed gurus of the high-consciousness movement. Biofeedback encourages the humanistic dream that the human being can become creator of his or her own health and healing.

This new interdisciplinary paradigm had emerged throughout the late 1960s, unifying developments from the diverse fields of psychology, neurophysiology, cybernetics, and medicine, culminating in a number of key publications in the final year of the decade. In 1969, Neal Miller, a psychologist specializing in brain and behavior at Yale and the Rockefeller Institute, published an article titled "Learning of Visceral and Glandular Responses." In 1966, brain researcher Elmer Green was senior author of "Self-Regulation of Internal States," and biofeedback was founded.

The contributions of many earlier researchers and practitioners can be cited as forerunners of biofeedback. Edmond Jacobsen commenced research at Harvard University in 1908, and throughout the 1920s and 1930s, he worked to develop progressive muscle relaxation (see the exercise earlier in this chapter) as an effective behavioral technique for the alleviation of neurotic tensions and many functional medical disorders. He used crude electromyography equipment to monitor the levels of muscle tension in his patients during the course of treatment.

The German psychiatrist Johannes Schultz contributed autogenic (a type of relaxation technique) training in the 1930s as a discipline for creating a deep, low-arousal condition with a pervasive quieting effect on the nervous system. B. F. Skinner, Albert Bandura, Joseph Wolpe, and others extended the operant training principles into a refined science of behavior therapy and behavior modification through instrumental learning. The building blocks were in place for a science of self-regulation by the 1960s.

The work of these pioneers allowed for the rapid application of biofeedback techniques. In 1986, Barry Sterman, a neurobiologist at UCLA, demonstrated that EEG- (or electroencephalogy, a test that measures brain waves) guided training of a specific sensor-motor rhythm over the sensor-motor cortex of the brain could suppress some epileptic seizures. In 1969, Elmer Green, a behavioral neuroscientist, reported on the use of self-regulation training for migraine headaches. In 1970, Thomas Budzynski, a psychologist and pioneer in the field of biofeedback, reported on the effects of feedback-induced muscle relaxation for tension headaches.

In 1974, neurobiologist Daniel Kohli used electromyography (EMG) feedback to teach patients to relax muscle groups and developed the concept of dysponses, or misplaced efforts, as a common neurophysiologic factor in many functional disorders. Many individuals facing stressful situations respond by dramatically increasing efforts in the same old directions and drawing on the same old strategies and habits. The result is a misplaced waste of effort and energy. In the face of stress, the individual engages in maladaptive muscular efforts, breathing patterns, and autonomic arousals producing illness and fatigue. As you have seen, the promise of biofeedback is to increase awareness of such dysponetic habits and to provide an avenue to new, healthier behavioral and physiological habits.

By 1975, the field of biofeedback had established a number of effective treatment protocols—for tension headaches, migraines, lower-back pain, tinnitus, temporomandibular disorders, hypertension, Raynaud's syndrome, incontinence, and a number of other functional disorders. The basic instrumentation triad of the electromyography (EMG), thermal feedback, and the galvanic skin response meter (GSR) had emerged as the workhorses of the biofeedback clinic. The EMG measures the electrical potential of muscle fibers, and it proved to be useful for general relaxation training, the treatment of headaches and muscular pain, and neuromuscular education. Thermal feedback measures skin temperature, especially finger temperature, and it demonstrated usefulness as an indirect measure of vasoconstriction or vasodilation and blood flow. Thermal feedback proved useful for migraine headaches, Raynaud's disease, hypertension, and general autonomic relaxation. The GSR, also referred to as a skin conductance or electrodermal activity meter, measures electrical changes in the skin, associated with sympathetic nervous arousal. The GSR became useful as an adjunct to psychotherapy and behavior therapy, measuring anxiety and cognitive-emotional threat reactions.

Mind-Body Medicine

Humanistic psychology dramatically emphasized the unity of mind and body. Renowned German-born psychiatrist and psychotherapist Fritz Perls introduced a number of body-awareness exercises into Gestalt therapy, as did the Reichian and other body-therapy schools into their disciplines. Biofeedback took this emphasis on a mind-body unity to a new level and created mind-body medicine. The psychophysiological principle was formulated in a variety of ways. Brain researcher Elmer Green and his associates expressed it as follows: "Every change in the physiological state is accompanied by an appropriate change in the mental-emotional state, conscious or unconscious, and conversely, every change in the mental-emotional state, conscious or unconscious, is accompanied by an appropriate change in the physiological state." Body and mind are one, and the pursuit of health requires a holistic, biopsychosocial approach.

Current applied psychophysiological methods can serve as a bridge between the traditional biomedical model and the biopsychosocial model in family medicine and primary care. More than 75 percent of patients visiting a primary-care physician present with physical symptoms related to psychosocial and behavioral factors. Psychiatrist George L. Engel called for a biopsychosocial model for medicine almost two decades ago, but this challenge remains unfulfilled.

A variety of these interrelated mind-body techniques—biofeedback, neurofeedback, hypnosis, and cognitive behavioral therapy—are effective tools for addressing an assortment of stress-related disorders and somatization (conversion of a mental state into physical symptoms) disorders. Psychophysiological assessment and psychophysiological monitoring using sophisticated electronic biofeedback and neurofeedback instruments can play a critical role in effective interventions with medical patients.

Combining Biofeedback with Mindfulness

Recently, the equipment being used for biofeedback has been modified and improved, and certain techniques, such as mindfulness, have been added as well. Mindfulness focuses on being in the moment and paying attention to your thoughts, feelings, and behaviors. Using mindfulness transformed my personal biofeedback work and that of my patients and my students.

Dr. Jon Kabat-Zinn, creator of the Center for Mindfulness in Medicine, Health Care, and Society, taught me to use the mindfulness approach with psychotherapy at his workshops and in his many wonderful articles and books. Mindfulness allows people to become truly aware of the present moment, tell the difference between what they can and cannot change, and then focus their attention on the things they can change.

After I analyzed the cases where biofeedback was not immediately successful, I realized that the reason for the lack of progress with biofeedback in some cases was that clinicians were teaching their patients to try to change things that were not changeable at that moment. I then realized that with mindfulness, I had a way to help my patients and my students get unstuck and make progress. My patients and I learned to allow what is outside of our control to stay and to apply our efforts to things we could control. The lesson here is that we cannot control what is outside of ourselves. The only things we can control are how we view our situation and how we handle it. It is not just what happens to us but how we deal with, look at, and resolve it.

Jon learned to change his intention by combining mindfulness with biofeedback. Along with his other concerns, he also had experienced chronic migraines. With biofeedback training, he learned to warm up his hands when he felt well, in order to bring the blood from the brain, where it had been creating the pain, to the hands. The biofeedback machine measured the temperature as it rose as Jon learned the skill of hand warming. However, every time Jon tried to warm up his hands when he was in pain, his finger temperature plummeted, his hands got colder, and his pain got worse. We figured out that he was trying to get rid of the pain by raising his finger temperature. His focus was on the numbers on the thermometer and on his level of pain. Using mindfulness, Jon learned to accept the pain he had at that moment and brought his focus to his image of warmth. As a result, his finger temperature rose, which began to bring relief from the pain of his migraines. Further work with his brain waves in neurofeedback complemented the biofeedback efforts, and Jon experienced a further and significant reduction in his migraines. (There will be more on this in the next chapter.)

Here are three reasons it can be useful to combine mindfulness with biofeedback.

1. **Sometimes people work hard to control what is out of their control.** Mindfulness can teach you to tell the difference between what is and is not controllable. Then you can choose to direct your resources toward creating the behavioral changes that are within your control.

2. **Sometimes we struggle to make the present moment be different.** Mindfulness gives us the freedom to choose our responses rather than following the automatic tendency to struggle. Rather than getting more nervous and upset, for example, we can accept what is in front of us and see our choices more clearly.

3. **Sometimes we judge ourselves for failing to reach our goals.** With mindfulness, we learn to give ourselves a break, to be kinder to ourselves. This mind-set then allows us to turn toward our experiences with curiosity and interest, and it gives us an opportunity to create change. We must be gentle with ourselves and learn to love ourselves. Every time we make a mistake, it is a lesson to learn something new. Ask yourself, "What can I learn from this experience?" and you will see what you must learn to do.

A Closer Look at Mindfulness

Christopher Germer, a clinical psychologist in Massachusetts and creator of mindful, passionate psychotherapy, took the literal translation of *mindfulness* from Pali, the language of the earliest Buddhist writings—that is, "awareness, remembering." Awareness is most relevant to the modern definitions of *mindfulness*, which is often described as simply moment-to-moment awareness. Jon Kabat-Zinn described it as "being in the present moment, accepting, and letting go of judgment."

In 2004, Ruth Baer and her colleagues at the University of Kentucky identified five facets of mindfulness, reflecting all of the major components of mindfulness practice and mindfulness interventions.

1. **Observing:** Attending to what is stimulating the person both internally and externally
2. **Describing:** Labeling one's experience with words
3. **Acting with awareness:** Choosing one's actions instead of behaving automatically, or being proactive, not reactive
4. **Taking a nonjudgmental stance:** Letting go of any judgment of one's external experience
5. **Practicing nonreactivity to internal experience:** Allowing thoughts and feelings to come and go without getting caught up in them

Acceptance is a concept closely related to mindfulness. Steven Hayes, the founder of acceptance and commitment therapy (ACT), describes it as "active, nonjudgmental embracing of experience in the here and now." Acceptance is also a way to live with your thoughts and feelings instead of struggling against them. It enables you to stop avoiding pain, both emotional and physical. It is what it is; acknowledge it.

How is all of this relevant to biofeedback? First, awareness is something that mindfulness and biofeedback share as a necessary component. In biofeedback, we first train our patients in awareness of their physiological sensations before they are able to learn and implement biofeedback skills. Mindful awareness of the present moment will make training awareness of physiological sensations easier. Second, a mindful approach will help the patient focus on what is most helpful about biofeedback. Third, integrating mindfulness into biofeedback practice allows us to work with what gets in the way of biofeedback success, such as: (1) automatic reactions to thoughts, feelings, and physiological sensations; (2) attempts to control or resist; and (3) judgment.

Mindfulness can help with the following:

- relaxation-induced anxiety (a condition in which being relaxed triggers anxiety)
- a sensation of being stuck
- pressure to get things just right
- feelings of distraction
- racing thoughts
- emotional reactions to physiological issues
- feelings of failure

Environmental Effects on Body-Mind Health

One trigger of physical and emotional symptoms that people often overlook is the environment. On this point, consider the stories of two of my clients, whom I'll refer to as Simone and Ricky.

One day, Simone came in to see me. She was a beautiful, tall blonde woman who was born in Helsinki, Finland. She could have easily been a model with that blonde, blue-eyed California look. She was a flight attendant and lived in Redondo Beach, close the Los Angeles International Airport, because she did so much traveling. Her presenting problem was a feeling of depression, daily physical pain, and loss of energy. Since I am not a medical doctor, I recommended that she go to a physician and have all the necessary tests to rule out any physical ailment that could have been contributing to her symptoms. She did see a doctor, and a month later, she came back to see me with all of her paperwork and blood tests, which ruled out many of the possible illnesses.

We started to talk, and Simone told me about where she was born and what it had been like to live there in Finland. I asked her if she thought the sunny and warm California weather could be a factor in her feeling unwell. She said that not one doctor had asked her that question and that it resonated with her. Soon thereafter, she and her husband made a decision to leave California and return to Helsinki.

Simone called me a month after resettling in Helsinki and said, "Dr. Singer, it is cold and snowing and raining and dark, and I feel wonderful—full of energy and alive, pain free, and happy. I thank you for all that you do." I told her she was welcome. The move made sense for her. Climate is an important aspect of where we live. A cactus cannot grow in an ocean.

Two weeks after that phone call, a young man named Ricky came to see me. Ricky was depressed and sad, and he had gone to see three different doctors. Each one had given him another drug to take. I asked Ricky to tell me about where he lived. He said he lived in an area that was nice but expensive. He had a basement apartment, which was below ground level. The apartment had no sunlight or fresh air, and it was claustrophobic at his place. I recommended that Ricky move. With some thought, Ricky decided a move was worth a try, and he found a new apartment. A month later, Ricky told me how great he felt. His mood was up, he felt happy with no depression, and he had lots of energy.

What lessons for us all! This is my approach to healing—to include mind, body, soul and spirit, and the environment!

The Chakras and How They Relate to Your Body

Chakras are energy centers located at various points in your body that allow you to live your life to its full expression and potential. The chakras are directly related to your body's overall health and your emotional well-being. Learning to activate and balance them is essential to your overall quality of life.

You can imagine each chakra as a rapidly spinning wheel of energy. There are seven chakras in your body, from the top of your head to the bottom of your spine.

> **Root Chakra:** The physical location of this chakra is at the base of the spine. It is associated with the color red and represents your foundation and your feeling of connection with the physical world.

Sacral Chakra: The second chakra is located along the spine in the lower abdomen, just below the navel. This orange-colored chakra represents our ability to feel connected with other people, to be accepting of others and open to new experiences.

Solar-Plexus Chakra: The third chakra is yellow in color. It sits along the spine in the upper abdomen. It reflects your personal power.

Heart Chakra: The fourth chakra is emerald green, and it is located next to the physical heart. It is the center of your ability to love and be loved.

Throat Chakra: The turquoise-colored fifth chakra is located in the throat. It represents your ability to communicate and express yourself.

Third-Eye Chakra: An indigo-colored chakra, the sixth chakra is located above the bridge of your nose, between your eyes. It supports intuition and your life path (your sense of purpose and direction).

Crown Chakra: The seventh chakra is the color violet. Located at the crown of your head, it supports your spirituality and unity with the divine.

The next exercise is a journey of balancing your colors and your chakra energy. All of the following colors in this exercise are the colors of the chakras. You can use gemstones or crystals during the chakra visualization to correspond with and represent each chakra; however, the most powerful chakra-harmonizing technique is to use your imagination!

I recommend that you read the following exercise into an audio recorder and play it back when you wish to do the exercise.

Exercise 3: Running the Chakra Colors

As you proceed, keep your breathing calm and regular, and use belly breathing.

Now see the color red. Fill your vision with the color red. Your entire consciousness becomes red. You see red and only red. You feel red; you taste red; you smell red; and you hear red. You are aware only of red. Your highest self selects the proper balance of red throughout all of your body.

Now the red fades away, and you become aware only of the color orange. You see the color orange. You fill your vision with the color orange. Your entire consciousness becomes orange. You see orange and only orange. You feel orange; you taste orange; you smell orange; and you hear orange. You are aware only of orange. Your highest self selects the proper balance of orange throughout all of your body.

Now the orange fades away, and you become aware only of the color yellow. You see the color yellow. You fill your vision with the color yellow. Your entire consciousness becomes yellow. You are yellow and only yellow. You feel yellow; you taste yellow; you smell yellow; and you hear yellow. You are aware only of yellow. Your highest self selects the proper balance of yellow throughout all of your body.

Now the yellow fades away, and you become aware only of the color green. You see the color green. You fill your vision with the color green. Your entire consciousness becomes green. You see green and only green. You feel green; you taste green; you smell green; and you hear green. Your highest self selects the proper balance of green throughout all of your body.

Now the green fades away, and you become aware only of the color turquoise. You see the color turquoise, you fill your vision with the color turquoise, and your entire consciousness becomes turquoise. You see turquoise and only turquoise. You feel turquoise; you taste turquoise; you smell turquoise; and you hear turquoise. You are aware only of turquoise. Your highest self selects the proper balance of turquoise throughout all of your body.

Now the green fades away, and you become aware only of the color turquoise. You see the color turquoise, you fill your vision with the color turquoise, and your entire consciousness becomes turquoise. You see turquoise and only turquoise. You feel turquoise; you taste turquoise; you smell turquoise; and you hear turquoise. You are aware only of turquoise. Your highest self selects the proper balance of turquoise throughout all of your body.

Now the turquoise fades away, and you become aware only of the color indigo (the color of blueberries, or bluish purple). You see the color indigo, you fill your vision with the color indigo, your entire consciousness becomes indigo, and you see indigo and only indigo. You feel indigo; you taste indigo; you smell indigo; and you hear indigo. You are aware only of indigo. Your highest self selects the proper balance of indigo throughout all of your body.

Now the indigo fades away, and you become aware only of the color violet (like the flower, or true purple). You see the color violet, you fill your vision with the color violet, your entire consciousness becomes violet, and you see violet and only violet. You feel violet; you taste violet; you smell violet; and you hear violet. You are aware only of violet. Your highest self selects the proper balance of violet throughout all of your body.

Now as the violet fades away, see yourself becoming at one with the universe. As you do, you see yourself becoming perfectly in harmony and in balance.

Now, as you prepare to return to your normal level of awareness, breathe deeply and pleasantly, and slowly open your eyes, stretching your body comfortably. Feel your body filling with health and loving energy.

Step 3: Brain

In the last chapter, you learned how biofeedback can help you learn self-regulation skills related to bodily responses. Neurofeedback is also training in self-regulation, and it is simply biofeedback applied to the brain directly. With neurofeedback, a person directly trains his or her own brain function, and the brain learns to function more efficiently. Neurofeedback is also called EEG neurofeedback because it is based on electrical brain activity noted by the electroencephalogram (EEG).

During a neurofeedback session, the practitioner observes the brain in action from moment to moment. He or she also shows the information to the person being monitored. The brain is then rewarded for changing its activity to more-appropriate patterns. This is a gradual learning process. It applies to any aspect of brain function that can be measured.

In essence, neurofeedback addresses the problems of brain dysregulation. These are many. They include the anxiety-depression spectrum, attention deficits, behavior disorders, various sleep disorders, headaches and migraines, PMS, and emotional disturbances. It is also useful for organic brain conditions, such as seizures, the autism spectrum, and cerebral palsy.

Working with Neurofeedback

Jon used neurofeedback to work with brain regulation. We targeted his presenting problems of anxiety, stress, sleep issues, and migraine headaches to be part of his treatment plan. With his work in neurofeedback along with biofeedback and therapy, he was able to feel less stressed and calmer, his sleep improved greatly, and there was a significant reduction in his migraines.

Like a muscle, your brain gets stronger the more you train it. Since your brain controls every nerve system, muscle, and organ in your body, when it works at maximum efficiency, you feel better and perform better. During neurofeedback treatment, technology is used to train your brain to correct faulty brain-wave activity. The process can be thought of as brain exercise.

Neurofeedback is on the forefront of the revolution in psychology being driven by the innovations in neuroscientific research. Integrating neuroscientific and psychotherapeutic treatments is the most effective path to psychological healing and growth, because the two approaches work synergistically to create a brain state that is most receptive to treatment.

Electrodes are applied to the scalp to listen in on brain-wave activity. Brain waves occur at different frequencies, from slow waves to fast waves, and each speed has its own function. Slow brain waves (delta and theta) reflect that the brain is underaroused or functioning at reduced capacity for mental efficiency. This state occurs during sleep or daydreaming, when areas of the brain go offline, so to speak, to take up nourishment. High levels of delta and theta in specific areas of the brain can also be associated with learning disabilities, depression, and inattention.

When the brain produces predominantly faster brain waves (alpha and beta), it is more fully aroused, alert, and focused. The neural networks are fully engaged to process information. Beta brain waves need to be dominant for controlling attention, behavior, organization, emotions, and basic learning functions. Too many fast waves in specific areas of the brain can cause anxiety, aggression, irritability, and other physical symptoms.

The computer processes the signals picked up by the electrodes to extract information about the key brain-wave frequencies. Information is presented to the person in the form of a video game or movie. The person is effectively playing the video game or watching the movie with his or her brain.

Eventually, the brain-wave activity is shaped toward more-desirable and more-regulated performance. The frequencies being targeted and the specific locations on the scalp where the practitioner listens in on the brain are specific to the conditions being addressed and specific to the individual person.

Neurofeedback is seldom used in isolation from other techniques. It is usual for the work with one's psychologist to include neurofeedback as well as biofeedback, mindful meditation, and/or cognitive behavioral therapy, along with exercises to support the changes a person will likely make in his or her life.

The Beginnings of Neurofeedback as a Discipline

In the early 1960s at the University of Chicago, psychologist Joe Kamiya made an interesting discovery about some of his research subjects. He noted that they could learn how to alter the power and speed of their brain waves if provided with information on the activity of their brains.

Neuroscientist Barry Sterman also did research involving neurofeedback in the late 1960s, at the University of California, Los Angeles. He found that cats could learn to alter their brain waves if they were given rewards for producing the goal brain wave. With repeated exposure to neurofeedback training, the cats became adept at doing so.

While these were remarkable discoveries, neurofeedback soon fell into disrepute for a number of reasons. First, some parties made claims for the technology that were not yet supported by science. Second, other involved parties formed links with flakier movements that compromised the scientific integrity of the discipline. Third, some in the scientific community and elsewhere thought that this technique was too close to mind control. The result was that neurofeedback was kept only barely alive by a few diehard pioneers until its revival in the 1980s.

The field of neurofeedback has grown rapidly, especially in the last ten years. The number of practitioners worldwide is approaching two thousand, with the bulk of those practitioners residing in the United States. There is a small scattering of practitioners across Canada. The field is beginning to recover from the low esteem in which it was formerly held; now the science is catching up with the claims that have been made for its efficacy. Even while new information is being collected and published, many health professionals—such as psychologists, psychiatrists, and family physicians—are unaware of current developments in the field.

The History of Quantitative Electroencephalography (QEEG)

Electroencephalography (EEG neurofeedback) has been studied and applied since the 1930s as a way of looking at the electrical functioning of the brain. Billions of neurons in the cortex, which are also influenced by structures beneath the cortex, produce electrical activity that is readable by attaching sensors to the scalp. The electroencephalograph amplifies those faint impulses so that the human eye can view them.

As digital computer technology developed in the 1960s and 1970s, scientists were able to more precisely examine a person's electrical brain functioning in ways not possible through simple visual inspection of raw brain-wave tracings. The computer can calculate and make visible many features of the EEG that the human eye cannot. This computer analysis of electroencephalography data and the associated behaviors is called quantitative EEG, or QEEG.

More on the Neurofeedback Experience

While the QEEG often reveals generalized problems in brain functioning that will influence many aspects of the individual's experience, people most often seek assistance from psychologists for a particular difficulty—the QEEG variable that most closely matches the complaint of the individual will be addressed first. Jon had suffered from migraines all of his adult life. He made progress with reducing the pain from his migraines through hand-warming exercises monitored with biofeedback. (There will be more on this in the last chapter.) The neurofeedback treatment twice a week for a half hour each session then helped his brain regulate and stabilize. He had taken many types of medications, but the stabilizing of the neural circuitry of his brain in neurofeedback, plus blood-flow work in biofeedback, was what helped him with the symptoms of migraines. By working on his brain waves, Jon also was able to focus more and be less distracted. The benefits of this intervention were outstanding. Because Jon was specific in reporting his symptoms, the clinician was able to precisely place the neurofeedback monitors. This enabled Jon to get the feedback he needed to be able to regulate his brain waves and thereby get the benefits.

On the basis of a strengths-and-weaknesses QEEG profile, the psychologist will choose a neurofeedback program to assist the individual in the learning process. The goal is the enhancement of strengths or, more often, the reduction or removal of weaknesses. For example, let's say that the QEEG assessment shows that an individual has too much slow activity (theta and delta) and not enough fast activity (beta) at the front of the brain. This person's complaint to the psychotherapist matches the complaint of frontal slowing. Then training might consist of inhibiting the slow (theta) activity and enhancing faster activity (beta).

The individual receiving neurofeedback training wears a clip on each ear, or one sensor on another place on the head, and one sensor on the site that has been targeted for training. The sensor that is designated as the target site is referred to as the active sensor. The brain-wave activity recorded by the active sensor is displayed on the computer monitor, perhaps as a colored bar or a moving line. In the example above, where the goal is to enhance faster activity (beta), the colored line represents beta and fluctuates up and down in accordance with the individual's own beta waves. Also visible on the screen is a threshold bar, set at an appropriate level such that beta activity is able to stay above it (exceed the threshold) at least 60 percent of the time. Each time the beta jumps over the bar (the beta recording reaches or exceeds the goal threshold set for it), the computer emits a tone. With repeated exposure to this form of feedback (that is, both visual and auditory), the brain begins to recognize a relationship between its own activity and what it is observing on the computer monitor. In other words, the brain begins to recognize its own mental states. This is when learning begins to take place.

Once the brain catches on to what it needs to do in order to make the line or bar successfully stay above the threshold a certain percentage of time and to hear the pleasant tone, it begins to do so more consistently. Although this sounds hard to believe, it has been established that this process helps most people learn how to control their own brain waves and, therefore, their own internal states. Fortunately, the changes are quantifiable and observable through measurements taken during the neurofeedback sessions, as well as through follow-up QEEG assessments.

In thinking about neurofeedback, it will be helpful to look at its associated learning in three ways:

1. Subconscious learning
2. The formation of a conscious association between feelings and brain states
3. The development of flexibility in neural pathways

Let's look at each of these more closely.

Subconscious learning occurs in the process whereby the brain, at a level below awareness, begins to recognize itself on the computer monitor and to make the changes required (such as related to the threshold bar). As this is occurring, the individual might feel disconnected from the process. People feel as though they are simply watching the display and listening to the tones, without experiencing it as a personal process driven by their own neural activity. This learning is on a subconscious level. Remember, cats and other animals can learn to alter their brain functioning when appropriate rewards are utilized—and they are not consciously considering what they need to do in order to receive the reward. In a similar way, the pleasant tone serves as a reward for human beings using this technology. The learning process occurs over time and outside the level of conscious awareness.

The second way that learning occurs is through conscious associations between indications that the target is being met (the visual and the auditory cues) and how the individual feels. Often, a description of how it feels to meet the target defies words. For example, many people are unable to express in words what "more alpha" feels like, although they can tell when it is occurring. This process of learning is conscious, and it involves the development of an awareness of sensations in one's body that were not present before. In this way, individuals are able to do voluntarily what is necessary in order to produce that sensation at will. There is the sense that "This is what it's supposed to feel like when I produce more alpha."

Finally, change through neurofeedback occurs as a result of exercising underdeveloped neural pathways. The more the brain practices moving into a more-optimal state, the more flexible it will be in responding to demands.

Tips for Finding the Right Neurofeedback Clinician

During a neurofeedback session, there is often nothing in particular that a patient can do but share the symptoms he or she is experiencing. Then the trained clinician can do his or her work. My bias is that the clinician should also be a therapist with training in psychology, cognition, and behavior.

If someone is interested in including this intervention in his or her treatment plan, my advice is to get a clinician trained in both biofeedback and neurofeedback, as well as psychology. I believe in treating the whole patient—mind, body, soul and spirit, and heart. Treatment is not just about the brain or the body, not just about your psychosis or your goals; it should focus on a holistic view of the entire person. At my Biofeedback Neurofeedback Treatment Center, we have been successful with our treatments when using this paradigm.

Be sure you ask your clinician about his or her training and treatment approach. Usually, therapists who focus on this orientation do cognitive behavioral therapy, but it would be best for you to ask about his or her academic preparation and treatment methods.

Step 4: Spirit and Soul

The meaning of life is to give life meaning.
—Viktor Frankl

What does it mean to be spiritual? It means that you are conscious of relating to your spirit and soul rather than just to the practical aspects of your physical reality.

Simply stated, spirit and soul are said to be separate yet connected entities. The soul is the essence of our inner being. It is the place inside us where inner peace and happiness are meant to reside. Spirit is the flow of energy that connects our soul with universal energy. This universal energy has been called universal knowledge, higher self, or even a form of energy called love. Spirit is the high-voltage power line that carries light (and love) to the soul.

Psychotherapy and spirituality meet when we go beyond basic psychological inquiry and look at higher states of awareness and a beyond-self way of being in the world. Spirituality might include religious expressions, but more often, it is recognized as a uniting force in the universe that lives within each of us, that draws us out and beyond our ego identification into the bigger world of creativity, mystery, and interdependence.

The integration of psychology and spirituality is an important component of personal growth, and this spiritual integration is here to stay. Being thoughtful of principles like respect, responsibility, integrity, competence, and concern for others will greatly help the psychology profession, manifesting this important aspect in treatment—spirituality and the journey within.

A spiritual connection can help you restore inner peace. For instance, this process can occur when you put your trust in the belief that a power greater than your own is available to assist you. It is simple to do, but you have to mean it. You also have to be willing to face yourself in the mirror and make the necessary changes, which is not easy and requires courage.

Dr. Frankl Tells Us to "Teach Spirituality"

In 1994, the Third Evolution of Psychology Conference took place in Hamburg, Germany. The keynote speaker was Austrian neurologist and psychiatrist Viktor Frankl. I attended his keynote with three of my doctoral psychology graduate students, and it was one of the most memorable and profound speeches I have ever heard. There were five thousand mental-health workers from all over the world in attendance. Dr. Frankl started his talk by saying, "Teach spirituality—it is the antidote to violence, emptiness, depression, and aggression." He stated that spirituality was not being taught to therapists, and therefore, therapists were not sharing it with their clients. He spent his whole address discussing the importance of spirituality.

His talk was mesmerizing, although I was already interested in spirituality in the 1990s. I had included that type of work with my patients because I had done extensive traveling and realized the importance of including Buddhism and other forms of spirituality in my practice, such as mindfulness, yoga, meditation, nature, and visualization.

Even so, this presentation by Frankl left a profound imprint on me. In the late 1980s, I had read about his amazing experiences as a concentration-camp survivor from World War II in his book *Man's Search for Meaning.* As a psychologist, I was riveted by his testament of the power of the human spirit to overcome even the most extreme circumstances imaginable. His ideas stirred a longing in me to live with courage, meaning, freedom, and love regardless of any circumstances and to teach meaning. Listening to Frankl speak of how he was able to transform his experience in the camp and become a better person was important to me.

Speaking to us in the Hamburg lecture hall, he said, "Ultimately, it is a choice—a choice to love and serve others, a choice to find meaning, a choice to have empathy for my captors, a choice to find gratitude in hell, a choice to find beauty, a choice even to find humor." His response is amazing.

As I reflect on his speech, it occurs to me that Frankl refused to allow his environment, his circumstances, or other people to dictate who he was and what he did. He was not a rat in a cage where stimulus and response ruled his existence. His example teaches that when we get to the point of being sick and tired of being sick and tired, we have a choice to connect with the marrow of our soul—that part that refuses to be captive, to live a life of reaction. This is the place where we choose freedom and growth, our existence in this moment, and who we will be. Ultimately, we have a choice to live from a place of internal liberation.

Frankl talked about how pain is different and real for each person individually. He talked about how one cannot compare his or her pain or experience to the pain of another. There comes a time in your life when you must force yourself to stop entertaining the trivial (the things you cannot control) and focus on the significant (the things you can control), namely yourself.

Since that year, 1994, I have reminded myself to live from that place of freedom and meaning. Daily, I share this message of growth, ownership, empathy, choice, meaning, gratitude, love, humor, and beauty with others, including my clients. Frankl could have come out of his experiences in the death camps with a vengeful, negative message full of anger, bitterness, and hate, but he chose not to. Yes, he *chose* not to. Instead, he chose to become a better person because of his experiences.

Frankl discussed what he believes success is. He believes that success is the influence and impact you have on others. Success is the difference you make for good in this world. As I listened to Dr. Frankl at the conference, in that moment, my soul and spirit were nourished and expanded in a way that I cannot describe. It was a learning moment for me to encounter this amazing being, and I am eternally grateful; I have carried his ideas forward and will continue to do so.

As a professor for over thirty years, I have told my students to keep growing and learning. Your patients see what you see, know what you know, and understand what you understand. They become aware to the point that you are aware. Listening to this speech guided me to experiences that took me to another level.

> Between stimulus and response, there is
> a space. In that space is our power
> to choose our response. In our response
> lies our growth and our freedom.
> —Viktor Frankl

The Journey to Find Meaning

There is another important message from Frankl's speech: "What man actually needs is not a tensionless state but rather the striving and struggling for some goal worthy of him. What he needs is not the discharge of tension, but the call of a potential meaning waiting to be fulfilled by him."

Frankl's story of how he survived the Holocaust focused on finding personal meaning in the experience, which gave him the will to live through it. He believes man's underlying motivator in life is a "will to meaning." Through his research, he found that there was a strong relationship between meaninglessness and criminal behaviors, addiction, and depression. Without meaning, people fill the void with hedonistic pleasures, power, materialism, hatred, boredom, or neurotic obsessions and compulsions. The ultimate meaning in life is a spiritual kind of meaning. Frankl focuses on finding meaning and fulfillment in life; he does not focus on the pursuit of happiness.

> Only when the emotions work in terms of values
> can the individual feel pure joy.
> —Viktor Frankl

In the pursuit of meaning, Frankl recommends three different courses of action:

1. Deeds
2. The experience of values through some kind of medium (e.g., beauty through art, or love through a relationship)
3. Suffering

While the third is not necessarily in the absence of the first two, within Frankl's frame of thought, suffering became an option through which to find meaning and experience values in life in the absence of the other two opportunities.

For Frankl, joy could never be an end to itself; however, it was an important by-product of finding meaning in life. He points to studies where there is a marked difference in life spans between "trained tasked animals" (i.e., animals with a purpose) and "taskless, jobless animals." Yet it is not enough simply to have something to do; rather, what counts is the "manner in which one does the work."

The Role of Responsibility

Frankl sees our ability to respond to life and be responsible in our work and other arenas as a major factor in finding meaning and, therefore, fulfillment in life. In fact, he viewed responsibility as the "essence of existence." He believed that humans were not simply the product of heredity and environment and that they had the ability to make decisions and take responsibility for their own lives and their impact on others. This element of decision is what Frankl believed made education so important.

The Value of Individuality

Frankl does not have a one-size-fits-all answer to the meaning of life. His respect for human individuality and each person's unique identity, purpose, and passions does not allow him to do otherwise. He encourages people to explore life and find their own unique meanings in it.

How do we do this? He quoted German author Goethe, who wrote, "How can we learn to know ourselves? Never by reflection, but by action. Try to do your duty and you will soon find out what you are. But what is your duty? The demands of each day."

The Discernment of Meaning

As human beings, we try to enlarge our discernment of meaning in three ways: (1) creatively, (2) experientially, and (3) attitudinally.

1. **Meaning through creative values.** This includes widening and broadening the visual field so that the whole spectrum of meaning and values becomes conscious and visible. A major source of meaning is the value of all we create, achieve, and accomplish.
2. **Meaning through experiential values.** Take a mountain climber who has beheld the alpine sunset and is so moved by the splendor of nature that he feels cold shudders

running down his spine, and ask him whether, after such an experience, his life can ever again seem wholly meaningless. (There will be more on this in the section "The Rapture of Nature" later in the chapter.)

3. **Meaning through attitudinal values.** We have the freedom to find meaning through meaningful attitudes, even in apparently meaningless situations. For instance, the following conversation helped my elderly, depressed patient who could not overcome the loss of her husband.

   I asked her, "What would have happened if you had died first and your husband would have had to survive you?"

   She replied, "For him, this would have been terrible; how he would have suffered!"

   I said, "You see, such suffering has been spared him, and it is you who has spared him this suffering. But now, you have to pay for it by surviving him and mourning him."

   She said nothing, but I saw in her eyes that the idea had taken hold. She shook my hand and calmly left the office.

Forgiveness and Its Role in Helping to Find Meaning and Purpose

Many of us do not get what we want in our lives, because we sabotage ourselves. We procrastinate. We resist. We don't follow through. We don't do the things we know are in our best interests. On some level, we do not love ourselves. The end result is a life that is unfulfilled and a disappointment. It does not have to be that way.

Our world changes for the better when we learn to love ourselves and eliminate the guilt, shame, and self-loathing deeply embedded in our unconscious minds (which generates our self-destructive and self-defeating behaviors). We start attracting people and circumstances that cooperate with our goals and propel us toward the manifestation of all of our hopes and dreams.

The way to eliminate our guilt, shame, and self-loathing is to value ourselves and forgive ourselves. The way to progress is to have a daily gratitude list and to have patience with ourselves.

By consistently practicing a daily regimen of thoughts, actions, and exercises devoted to accepting ourselves, forgiving ourselves, and being of service to others, our self-esteem increases, our self-sabotaging behaviors decrease, and we experience greater opportunities and more-positive outcomes in all areas of our lives.

Later in the chapter, there will be a mindful meditation for forgiveness.

The Chakras and How They Relate to Your Life

In step two, "Body," you were introduced to the chakras—energy centers located at various points in your body. Stress, depression, bodily injury, or pain can cause one or more of your chakras to become clogged and out of balance, which will adversely affect the flow of energy. If energy cannot flow openly and freely through all of your chakras, you'll experience problems associated with the blockage.

Chakra meditation is used to help reestablish the balance of your chakras to restore the free flow of energy (for examples, see the next section below). Those who have not practiced any chakra meditation before can perform their usual form of meditation to prepare themselves for it.

Imagine the flow of chakra energy as a river. When the river is free of obstacles, the water flows smoothly and steadily, nourishing life along the banks. The free flow of energy from the chakras nourishes your organs and other bodily functions; your chakras are the emotional, mental, and spiritual aspects of yourself.

Now, if you were to start tossing rocks into the river—emotional distress, negative thoughts, and life stress—you would start to create disturbances in the flow. If enough rocks accumulated in certain areas, the flow of energy could be slowed drastically or even stopped altogether. That means life upstream and life downstream are negatively affected—some areas have too much energy, while others starve.

The colors associated with each chakra are important. Colors, like everything else in the universe, have a unique energetic (vibrational) signature. This means that when you go about clearing blockages in certain chakras, you will want to keep their colors in mind. You can use color-related gemstones or crystals, if available, during the chakra meditation to correspond with and represent each chakra.

Let's review the seven chakras and their colors, locations, significances, and possible associated disturbances.

Root Chakra. Located at the base of the spine, this chakra is associated with the color red and represents your foundation and your feeling of connection with the physical world. You have a blockage in this chakra if you experience recurring financial problems (in the modern age, money is a symbol of survival and security). You might feel tired and run down. You might feel stuck in a job that you hate, where you feel unfulfilled and inadequately rewarded. You might experience adrenal fatigue (from too much stress), eating disorders, and bone disorders.

Sacral Chakra. Located along the spine in the lower abdomen, just below the navel, this chakra is associated with the color orange and represents our ability to feel connected with other people, to be accepting of others and open to new experiences. Your sacral chakra is blocked or weakened if you have any sexual problems (i.e., you don't feel sexy or attractive; you have a low libido); have difficulty in relationships; or repeatedly attract the wrong types of people.

Solar-Plexus Chakra. Located along the spine in the upper abdomen, this chakra is associated with the color yellow and reflects your personal power. The third chakra is blocked if you lack self-confidence and self-esteem; frequently feel embarrassed by what others think of you; feel like a victim; or suffer from stomach pains and stomach anxiety.

Heart Chakra. Located next to the physical heart, this chakra is associated with the color emerald green and represents your ability to love and be loved. Your fourth chakra is blocked if you have trouble opening up to others; feel clingy and needy; experience heart problems, asthma, or allergies; or feel unable to accept yourself.

Throat Chakra. Located in the throat, this chakra is associated with the color turquoise and represents your ability to communicate and express yourself. Your fifth chakra is blocked if you have problems being honest; feel you cannot speak up and voice your needs or opinions; or suffer from sore throats, sinus problems, or dental problems.

Third-Eye Chakra. Located above the bridge of your nose, between your eyes, this chakra is associated with the color indigo—the color of blueberries, or bluish purple. It supports intuition and your life path—your sense of purpose and direction. Your sixth chakra is blocked if you feel lost, wondering, *Why am I here? Why was I even born?* and you can't make decisions without second-guessing yourself. Also, if you have sinus troubles and frequent headaches, then there can be blockages here.

Crown Chakra. Located at the crown of your head, this chakra is associated with the color violet—like the flower, or true purple. On a spiritual level, it supports your spirituality and unity with the divine. On a physical level, it supports the nervous system and brain functions. Your seventh chakra is blocked if you feel lonely; feel insignificant; feel worthless; or get headaches and experience neurological issues.

The Chakras and Our Health

The modern world in which we all live can be a baffling, stressful, and exhausting place. For centuries before our generation, people lived with a closer connection to the earth around them, and they relied more on their friends and families for support. If we recognize that we are suffering mentally or spiritually, modern doctors are likely to prescribe a range of medicines that change the way we think, and this attempt to solve issues solely with medication encourages us to ignore our sadness, frustration, or desperation. These methods might be effective in one sense, but they fail to see the body as more than simply the sum of its parts. They fail to recognize the importance and the existence of the spirit or the way in which the body produces, uses, and transmits energies in order to keep us healthy and motivated. In addition, modern living and modern healing ignore the source of problems and illnesses, leaving them more than likely to return in some form or another.

This was not always the case, and more and more people are awakening to this truth. Those in the Eastern world have always seen the body, mind, and spirit as fundamentally entwined realities, and they continue to view problems, illnesses, or difficulties, such as depression and frustration, as the result of blocked or leaking energies. The wisdom of ancient cultures from countries like India and China has survived through writings and practices, and it is now more available to the general public all over the world, thanks to the advent of the Internet. In India particularly, thousands of years of careful examination of the human body and spirit resulted in a deep knowledge of the passage of energies through the physical form, something that not only has formed the basis for much of the subcontinental Asian culture but also is being embraced with open arms by the Western world today.

Many people are turning to the wisdom of India—whether through yoga classes, healing sessions, or chanting—and other Eastern countries to fill the void that Western society and culture has left in their hearts. This void has begun to damage us. We see an ever-increasing list of physical and mental complaints in the Western world, which have come about as a result of our detached and spiritless lifestyles, and we are longing for a more holistic way to integrate Eastern concepts into our ways of thinking, teaching, healing, and being in the world.

For many of us, this interest comes about from a greater understanding of how our bodies work and how we are able to effectively and enjoyably heal ourselves by seeing our physical forms in their entirety. But this is not the whole story. We must also look to our minds and spirits not as entities separate or detached from our physical bodies but as important components that are essential aspects of ourselves. Should our minds or spirits become sick or slow, we should no longer express surprise at how this causes our bodies to become unwell.

In an interesting way, we have always known the importance of integrating these ideas into our ways of being. We often associate stress or heartbreak with physical symptoms, such as ulcers or high blood pressure, but many of us are hesitant to take this logic further. With knowledge of how our energy works and how it flows and cycles through our bodies, we can begin to unlock the secrets of how to cure our ills and live stronger, healthier, happier, and more confident and empowered lives.

Clearing Blockages in the Chakras

Our bodies have hundreds of energy centers within them, tempering, controlling, pushing, transmitting, and receiving energy from the inside to the outside and vice versa. However, we have seven key energy centers (as described above) within us—those large ones known as the chakras. These chakras (translated as "wheels" or "vortex" in Sanskrit) are powerful, pulsing centers of energy that run in a straight line through the center of our bodies. Beginning at our tailbones and ending at the tops of our heads, these chakras are connected to both the earth below us and the heavens above, and they ground us and inspire us in equal measure.

Each chakra is responsible for not only providing our bodies with the energy required to function happily and healthily but also ensuring that our emotional lives are running in a positive direction, we can feel and understand our connection with the divine, we can find and utilize our true voices and inspiration, and we can freely and creatively follow our paths in life. As such, it is vitally important—not just for our physical health but also for our all-around, holistic health—to ensure that our chakras are well looked after and kept open and unblocked.

Let's move on to clearing the blockages and restoring harmony. Clearing the chakra blockages involves using your intention and visualization. The best approach is to be open to receiving spiritual guidance so that you're making the most-effective strides toward harmonizing and balancing your energy systems.

Clearing and balancing your chakras is something you'll want to do at least twice a year, if not more often. Your physical, emotional, mental, and spiritual needs change constantly as new challenges come up.

There are various ways to vitalize your chakras for better energy health. Here's an easy one: when there's an energy leak, you have to patch it. This can relate to a certain area of your life and the associated chakra. Also, many people are energy depleted because they're not able to hold enough life-force energy, or chi. In this energy condition, you're flushing energy down and away from you.

In order to maintain good energy health, you want energy spiraling up from your base chakra. Try the following.

Exercise 1: Base-Chakra Patching

- Close your eyes, and imagine that you can see the energy leaking out of your tailbone.
- Imagine a patch large enough to cover the leak.
- Place the patch over the leak.
- Imagine that you can go beneath the energy and reverse the flow to spiral it up into your body through your tailbone.

Life-force energy is also fed to us through our crown chakra. The crown chakra is located on the top of your head. We maintain higher life-force energies when our crown chakras are open and active. When the crown chakras are closed or weak, we feel a lack of vitality and direction in our lives. As a result, we look to others rather than to our own spiritual compasses for guidance.

Try the following.

Exercise 2: Opening the Crown Chakra

- Place the fingertips of each of your hands on the top of your forehead, where your hairline starts. Your fingertips from each hand should be touching.
- Now pull your fingertips away from each other as though you were opening up your crown.

- Move your fingers two inches above the starting point, and repeat the same movement.
- Do this over the entire crown of your head. Take three deep breaths to anchor in this opening.

Disruption of the flow of your life-force energy occurs when a chakra is frozen or weak. It's common for an individual to have a frozen or weak third chakra, the solar-plexus chakra. The third chakra represents your will, power, confidence, and sense of self. This results in a lack of confidence or will to move forward enthusiastically.

Try the following.

Exercise 3: Strengthening the Solar-Plexus Chakra

- Rub your palms together swiftly, creating static electricity.
- Place the palm of your right hand on your solar plexus (along the spine in your upper abdomen), and rotate your palm in a clockwise direction while repeating, "I am powerful. I am the will for creating what I want."
- Repeat these steps two or three more times.

Your chakra energy is one of your most powerful and important energy systems. Working with these energy systems will bring energy and harmony to your life.

Mindful Meditation

Daily meditation is a life changer. Meditation radically improves our well-being—psychologically, spiritually, physically, and emotionally. Jon realized that he had to add meditation to his daily regimen, and it helped him balance his energies.

The following are mindful-meditation practices for various purposes.

Exercise 4: Relaxation

Put on some calming instrumental music. Find a comfortable position to sit in, somewhere quiet. Close your eyes, and take a deep breath. Gently exhale, count down from twenty, and let yourself sink into a relaxed state of mind. To go deeper into this state, start with a gentle relaxation of your physical body. Move your focus down your body, part by part, and relax each section completely as you go. Feel that feeling of relaxation flow all the way to your toes. For a more-extensive progressive-relaxation exercise, see exercise 1 in "Step 2: Body."

Exercise 5: Connection

Focus on your consciousness. Picture it as a white light surrounding your entire body in a bubble of peaceful, gentle, loving energy. Imagine this light expanding to connect you to your entire neighborhood, city, country, continent, and planet. Feel that sense of oneness. See yourself for what you are: a piece of consciousness directly connected to every other life-form on planet Earth.

Exercise 6: Gratitude

Bring to mind five to ten things you're truly grateful for, big or small. Express gratitude for these things. Vividly recall how they make you feel. Use all five senses: smell, touch, taste, sound, and vision. Feel this gratitude vibrate throughout your body. Know that when you express gratitude for beautiful moments in life, you open the way for these moments to repeat themselves and grow in terms of their magnitude.

When Jon wanted to discuss using the five senses with gratitude, I told him to tell me what he was most thankful for. He then started to talk about his excellent health.

I asked him, "What does that smell like to you?"

Jon answered, "It smells like fresh grass just cut."

"And what is the touch of your health like?" I further prompted.

"Soft and strong," he said.

"And how does it taste and sound?"

Jon stated, "It's like a freshly squeezed fruit juice, and the sound is like the sound of a harp."

"What does it look like?"

"The vision is of a gorgeous spring meadow."

Your senses vibrate on all five levels to touch you deeply. Once you have learned to meditate and connect to these deep experiences, it becomes joyful to do this exercise.

Exercise 7: Forgiveness

Bring to mind anyone whom you have had a conflict with. Imagine that person in front of you. Apologize for any wrong that you brought to him or her. Ask for his or her forgiveness. Forgive the person for any wrong that he or she brought to you. Feel that feeling of forgiveness throughout your body, and forgive yourself as well. Know that on a deeper level, we are one, and any negative charge toward any other living person is a charge against yourself. So forgive yourself as well.

Exercise 8: Visualizing Your Perfect Future

Visualize all the different aspects of your life as you want them to unfold in the future. Be as vivid as possible, and incorporate all five senses: taste, touch, smell, sound, and vision. As you wrap up the meditation, mentally tell yourself, *Let this or something better unfold in my life.*

Exercise 9: Daily Intention

Visualize yourself from the current moment, living the best version of this particular day. Make the scene as vivid as possible. Bring in emotions of joy and excitement. Bring yourself to the end of your day. See yourself going to bed and entering into a deep, comfortable, and rejuvenating sleep. Visualize yourself making the next day amazingly wonderful, too.

Exercise 10: Blessing

Call on any higher power you believe in, which could be your own inner strength. Ask for energy, support, and help in crafting your best day so that you can make your dreams for your future unfold. Feel this support, harmony, and energy all around you, protecting you and embracing you. Know that love is on your side and that a universe filled with love surrounds and supports you.

At the end of any one of these meditations, bring yourself slowly out of your meditation by counting upward from one to five. Your day is about to restart in a wonderful way, and all your amazing, rapturous dreams and visions for your future are coming to you.

When you go through your meditations, avoid frustration! Roll with it, and relax into the world of your imagination, where there are no limits. Nothing can exist in your imagination that you don't place there yourself. If you imagine energy flowing freely through the chakras—and if that is your intention—it will happen!

The Rapture of Nature

Jon brought up spirituality in our therapy sessions. He thought it had to do with religion, and he mentioned that religion had not been a focus in his family as he grew up. Then, a little later, Jon mentioned how much he loved surfing. He would get up in the early morning to go down to the beach and look at the ocean, studying the swells, the movement, and the beauty of the waves.

Jon said he felt a shudder going through him during the sunrises and the moments of pure bliss that he experienced during those times. This is an example of what the rapture of nature means to a being. It is indescribable ecstasy. Jon told me that when he was surfing and in the tube of a wave, he felt he was in the cradle of God.

I mentioned to Jon that this was spirituality, that this was his religion. He understood this concept at the depths of his being. So in addition, the word *spirituality* can be expanded to include nature. There needs to be a greater awareness of nature as a means of righting the imbalances that exist in our deepest selves and our environment.

Advice from a Tree
by Ilan Shamir

Dear Friend,
Stand tall and proud
Sink your roots deeply into the Earth
Reflect the light of a greater source
Think long term
Go out on a limb
Remember your place among all living beings
Embrace with joy the changing seasons
For each yields its own abundance
The energy and birth of spring
The growth and contentment of Summer
The wisdom to let go of leaves in the Fall
The rest and quiet renewal of Winter

Feel the wind and the sun
And delight in their presence
Look up at the moon that shines down upon you
And the mystery of the stars at night.
Seek nourishment from the good things in life
Simple pleasures
Earth, fresh air, light
Be content with your natural beauty
Drink plenty of water
Let your limbs sway and dance in the breezes
Be flexible
Remember your roots
Enjoy the view!

Bristlecone Pines by Dr. Lita Rawdin Singer, copyright 2001

As I started to write this book, I knew I wanted to include the delightful poem "Advice from a Tree" by Ilan Shamir. He is a writer who is obviously tuned into what nature has to offer us on a spiritual level. At age eleven, instead of a brightly wrapped gift, train, or puppy, he got a magnolia tree for his birthday. Growing up with the tree, he considered it his friend. Later in life, during a difficult time, he asked a hundred-year-old cottonwood tree for advice. The down-to-earth messages he received were captured in his poem, which reminds us of the restorative aspects of the spirit of nature.

The black-and-white image of the 4,500-year-old tree in the White Mountains of California is also powerful. This forest is still alive because the trees learned to be resilient. Despite the rough conditions of dry soil, extreme winds, and cold temperatures, they have survived like Frankl. Their adaptation was to grow slowly. Today the bristlecone pine is the oldest type of tree on Earth.

Here's the story behind the photo. I was prepared to go on my third trip to Tibet on September 12, 2001, with three photographers. But 9/11 happened, and we were unable to go there. So we decided to visit this amazing place in the White Mountains, and I photographed it. Immersing ourselves in the rapture of nature while enduring the devastation that our nation was experiencing was healing.

Nature has always inspired me. I have always enjoyed hiking through pristine forests and across savannas, making a connection to the natural world. This passion for nature continues for me to this day.

I have traveled all over the world and met shamans and healers. The indigenous consciousness holds the key not only to understanding our most primal selves but also to healing issues at the deepest level of self. These native peoples seem to have found the balance that we in modern society have lost. I believe that Westerners need to find pure exposure to the wilderness. A trip to the wilderness, while keeping as little as possible between nature and us, can help us tap into a different spiritual dimension.

The movement toward the inner world is our primary purpose on the planet. If we deviate from our soul's path, we create imbalance and poor health. Each individual must find the healer and healing technique that best connects him or her to self. Experiences in nature aid in self-restoration, and this becomes an inner meditation, not an outer striving.

Wilderness rapture is a term that captures what happens when you're in the wilderness. When you're there with the right intention, you get into a state of total harmony—a sense of wonder, awe, and inner peace comes over you.

For a major birthday celebration, I decided to take my family, including children and grandchildren, on an eight-day rafting trip down the 277-mile Colorado River in the Grand Canyon. Before this trip, my grandchildren sometimes asked me where I prayed and what temple I attended, so I wrote them a letter and included it in our orientation packet for the rafting adventure. It told them, "Nature is my cathedral. This is where I feel united completely with the universe." For them, it was a trip of a lifetime—full of rapture. They were blissful, peaceful in harmony with their own energy and that of the universe surrounding them.

That trip was ten years ago, and my children and grandchildren still talk about the wonder, magic, and ecstasy of that experience. It was similar to the stages of the archetypical hero's journey. The hero's journey puts us in contact with an experience that is going to challenge us in some fundamental ways. During the Grand Canyon river-rafting trip, we faced rapids that were coded as tens. I even said to myself, *What am I doing here?* This is not to say that when we go out into the wilderness, we will experience a terrifying ordeal in which we will be in some physical danger. Yet when we embark on such a journey, there is the potential for peril. We have the sense that we are entering this magical space where there are possibilities for danger. In this way, nature reflects our daily lives. It is how we navigate the journey—and possible dangers—that makes the difference.

Without contact with nature, there is something missing—it is like a type of soul death, like losing a loved one, as if a part of oneself is gone.

Exercise 11: Gaining an Inner Passage through Nature

What can someone who doesn't have the resources or the courage to go deep into the wilderness do to gain an inner passage through nature? Perhaps first try going into a garden. Look, feel, smell, touch, dig in the mud, run barefoot in the grass, and enjoy it for no reason but because it is there. That will be a healing experience.

Or appreciate trees. In the leaves of trees, we can observe every aspect of the life cycle. Go to the poem "Advice from a Tree," and then read it while *feeling* it. Next, go to local parks, or join area hikes. Once you have increased your confidence level, go on a weekend jaunt into the great outdoors. It's just a question of taking a leap of faith and adopting an attitude, an intention, of receptivity. If you do this in a Zen-like way, quietly opening to the inner healing experience, you will open your heart to the nature that is all around you and a part of you.

Step 5: Heart

I then looked into my heart
and it was there where He dwelled that I saw him;
He was nowhere else to be found.

— Rumi

Most of us don't understand the heart. The heart is one of the masterpieces of creation. It is a phenomenal instrument. It has the potential to create vibrations and harmonies that are far beyond the beauty of pianos, violins, or flutes. You can hear an instrument, but you *feel* your heart. And if you think that you feel an instrument, it is only because it touched your heart. Your heart is an instrument made of subtle energy that few people come to fully appreciate.

The Poetry of Rumi

Caught in the Fire of Love

My heart is on fire!
In my madness
I roam the desert
The flames of my passion
Devour the wind and the sky

My cries of longing
My wails of sorrow
Are tormenting my soul

You wait
Patiently
Looking into my intoxicated eyes
You accept my passion
With the serenity of love
You are the master of existence

One day I shall be
A Lover like you.

—Rumi

It was a lovely fall evening in Santa Barbara. Our poetry class was sitting on the comfortable leather couches on the second floor in the Fireside Room of the beautiful gothic Trinity Episcopal Church. Fariba, our poetry teacher, was reciting this Rumi poem in Farsi, while downstairs, the men's choir was rehearsing their program for Sunday's mass. The men's music sounded like the Gregorian chants. This moment was extraordinary—the sounds, the sights of the beautiful church, the feeling of wonder reverberating in every part of my being. What a moment! What a blessing! What a gift!

Every Monday evening, we met, and under the guidance of Fariba, we felt, heard, and experienced what this amazing poet who lived eight hundred years ago had to share.

Rumi's work was not new to me; I had been reading his poetry for many years. In fact, I'd been giving copies of these poems to my patients and had noticed extraordinary changes occurring as a result. People came to me trying to find their inner peace, inner guidance, and, most of all, self-love. I had seen that love was what had been missing for most of the people who sought therapy with me. Self-loathing, guilt, shame, and negativity abounded. Through Rumi's poetry, my patients were finding meaning and opening their hearts.

In addition to her poetry classes, Fariba was also pursuing her doctorate, and her dissertation was "Rumi's Poetry: The Journey toward Meaning and Transformation." Her research, which examined how Rumi's poetry impacts the lives of individuals who study his teachings, found a similar profound effect in her study subjects.

Fourteen experienced students and fourteen students who were new to the study of Rumi participated in Fariba's study. She used a grounded analytical approach to analyze the new students' reflections written during a study workshop, as well as in-depth interviews with all students. The findings show that the students were searching for more meaning and understanding of themselves and their lives. As they engaged with the core concepts of Rumi's poetry, they felt validated and comforted by the affirmation they received. Students were able to understand themselves and others better, and they found deeper meaning in their lives.

For those of you who are not familiar with the thirteenth-century Persian poet and Sufi mystic Rumi, I will give you some background.

Who Is Rumi?

Rumi was born on September 30, 1207, in a town located in what is currently Afghanistan. He was given the name Jalâluddin Muhammad, which translates to "Glory of Religion." He grew up in the Persian city of Balkh, important then for both commerce and intellectual pursuits. Fifty-six at the time of Rumi's birth, his father, Bahaduddin Walad, was a learned theologian, noted lecturer, scholar, preacher, and mystic. In fact, it is said that preaching had been a family business for generations. Bahaduddin Walad was also a disciple of the influential Sufi Najm al-Din Kubra. In addition to his father and Sufi teachers, it is believed that other influences on Rumi as he grew up and became a man were the Persian poets Attar and Sanai.

After the Mongols invaded, Rumi and his family eventually settled in another part of the Persia Empire (now Konya, Turkey). The area was along the Silk Road and was a place where people of different faiths—Muslims, Christians, Hindus, and travelers who were Buddhist—are believed to have associated with each other. Upon his father's death, Rumi himself became an important spiritual teacher.

Later, Rumi's life changed dramatically. The shift occurred after he met Shams-e Tabrizi on November 15, 1244. In contrast to Rumi, with his life of privilege and reputation, Shams was a wandering monk with rough ways and no formal schooling. Yet the two connected on a profound spiritual level. Over a period of two years, they went on a series of retreats and spent much time together exploring deep spiritual inquiries.

Jealousies developed, and feeling the resentment from Rumi's followers and family, Shams went into exile numerous times. Shams was eventually murdered after one of his reappearances. While Rumi was devastated by the loss, this friend would forever be a part of his life, based on Shams's influence during their time together. The ideas that grew from their association also live on to the present day in Rumi poems, including the concept of how we make contact with God—through love and the heart.

On December 17, 1273, Rumi died in Konya. While he wrote for most of his life, his poems grew richer after he met Shams. His major works include *Maṭnawīye Ma'nawī* (*The Spiritual Couplets*), encompassing six volumes of poetry, and *Dīwān-e Shams-e Tabrīzī* (*The Works of Shams of Tabriz*), a massive collection of Persian couplets and quatrains, named after his friend Shams. A wonderful source of his work today is the compilation *The Essential Rumi*, from renowned Rumi translator Coleman Barks and his associates. It is the best selling of all Rumi books.

About fifteen years ago, the Turkish Psychological Association invited me to go to Turkey to speak to the people who had pulled out the bodies of the deceased after a major earthquake. I ended up in Konya per chance and visited the amazing Mevlana Museum, the memorial to Rumi. There I met many mourners who were followers of Rumi, and I had some enchanting connections with them. The complex also houses the lodge of the dervishes of the Mevlevi order, and their breathtaking, swirling dances to the somber music resonated throughout my body, as Rumi's poetry does for me. Since Rumi's passing in 1273, the Mevlevi dervishes have honored him with their dancing to help others achieve a greater sense of the divine.

Rumi as a Phenomenon

Rumi's poetry is available in many languages today, including Farsi, Spanish, French, German, Italian, Turkish, and English, and he has fans and devotees around the world, breaking through ethnic and religious barriers. In 2014, the BBC dubbed him "the most popular poet in the US," noting that millions of copies of his work have sold in America in recent years. He is often thought of as the greatest mystical poet of any age.

Rumi's work and its call for respect for all people despite their religion or station in life drew criticism in Rumi's time, especially from strict followers of religious dogma. He invites his readers to seek spiritual freedom and turn away from fear-inducing creeds.

His themes include philosophy, personal growth, cultural assumptions, and, especially, love in all of its dimensions, from heated desire to soul-touching companionship. Interestingly, he talks about God in some of his poems and then dismisses God in many others. His primary message is that God is found in your own heart. He wrote all of these pieces with a unique universality. His poems convey the heart and mind of an evolved spiritual being.

What is it about Rumi's poetry that is so compelling that it has the capacity to open hearts? This question in particular interests me because people who come into my office today are involved in law, engineering, information technology, and insurance—fields that require them to rely primarily on the intellectual-thinking part of themselves. What these folks need is the ability to open their hearts, tap into their feelings, and experience that other part of their being. Rumi is able to reach them, even those who never liked poetry. In part, I believe this universality is because over his long, creative life, Rumi addressed virtually every topic; hence, he can become like a mirror, projecting what is in the reader's own mind. In addition, he speaks from the heart and is not overly intellectual.

A client of mine, Cynthia, who worked in IT for one of the largest insurance companies, was bright and aware but cut off emotionally. Yet she was responsive to a poem I gave to her. She read it to me and cried when I first gave it to her.

I told her, "Describe what was going on in you."

Cynthia responded, "I am so touched; my heart is aching and feels warm and loving, and that is what I am experiencing now. I have never felt so many deep emotions, Dr. Singer, and I think it is because I am feeling and not thinking as I usually do."

I also enjoy working with Rumi poetry with my clients because many find his work to have a lot of layers. They discover more in the poems as time goes on. Later, Cynthia told me, "The more I read Rumi's poetry, the more aware and conscious I become of my personal process and the depth of my being." She said that the poet Rumi had become an important spiritual guide for her journey within.

Many clients say, "How do I start? What do I do to open my heart?" From my experience and what I have witnessed, my recommendation is to introduce yourself to the poetry of Rumi.

Wherever you go,
Go with all your heart.
—Confucius

Opening the Spiritual Heart

In most humans, the heart does its work unattended. Even though its behavior governs the course of our lives, it is not understood. If at any given point in time the heart happens to open, we fall in love. If it happens to close, the love stops. If the heart happens to hurt, we get angry, and if we stop feeling it altogether, we experience a sense of emptiness. All of these different sensations happen because the heart goes through changes. These energy shifts and variations that take place in the heart are what run our lives. We are so identified with them that we use words like *I* and *me* when we refer to what's going on in our hearts. But you are not your heart. You are the experience of your heart.

Your heart is an energy center, a chakra—the heart chakra. This is one of the most beautiful and powerful energy centers, and it affects your daily life. An energy center is an area within your being through which your energy focuses, distributes, and flows. This energy flow has been referred to as Shakti, chakra, spirit, and chi, and it plays an intricate part in your life. You feel the heart's energy all the time. Think about what it is like to feel love in your heart. Think about what it's like to feel inspiration and enthusiasm pour from your heart. Think about what it's like to feel energy well up in your heart, making you confident and strong. All of these feelings happen because the heart is an energy center.

The heart controls the energy flow by opening and closing. This means that the heart, like a valve, can either allow the flow of energy to pass through, or it can restrict the flow of energy from passing through. If you observe your heart, you know what it feels like when it is open and what it feels like when it is closed. For instance, you can experience great feelings of love while in the presence of someone, until he or she says or does something you don't like. Then your heart closes toward the person. You simply do not feel the love anymore. What causes this phenomenon?

What is it about the structure of the heart center that permits it to close? The heart closes because it becomes blocked by stored, unfinished energy patterns from your past. You need to examine your everyday experiences to understand why you are closed. As events happen, they come in through the senses and have an impact on your inner state of being. They can bring up fear, anxiety, or maybe love. Your senses are electronic sensing devices. If the energy patterns coming into your psyche create disturbance, you'll resist them and not allow them to pass through you. When you do this, the energy patterns get blocked within you.

It's important to understand what it's like to have these energies stored within you. What would it be like if nothing were stored? If everything passed right through you, as you were driving down a highway and passing thousands of trees, they wouldn't leave an impression on you. They would be gone as soon as you perceived them. Although they would come in through the senses and make impressions on your mind, you would release them. You would have no personal issues with them.

This is how the overall system of perception is meant to work. It is meant to take things in, allow you to experience them, and then let them pass through so that you are fully present in the next moment. The trees, the road, and all that you see are experiences passing through you, awakening and stimulating you.

What it means to live life is to experience the moment that is passing through you and then experience the next moment and then the next. Many different experiences will come in and pass through you. Perception is a phenomenal system when it is working properly. If you could live in that state, you would be a fully aware being. Full awareness is how awakened beings live in the now. They are present, life is present, and the wholeness of life passes through them. Imagine if you were so fully present during each experience of life that life was touching you to the depth of your being; every moment would be a stimulating, moving experience, because you would be completely open. Life would be flowing right through you.

But this is not what happens inside most of us. As you are driving down the street, you see the trees and the cars, and then, inevitably, something comes along that brings trouble. You see a car that looks like your former friend's car, someone you have past issues with. Your heart and mind become blocked, this event gets stuck, and that is what you are focusing on. The inner noise starts in your mind, and you are not present. In your mind, you're trying to figure things out. An impression from the past—an unfinished energy pattern—ends up running you. These are the things we need to work on outside and within our therapeutic relationships in order to clear them away. They call this stored past-energy pattern at your heart center a samskara. These patterns are the blockages that can produce a state of depression. Dark energy is coming into your heart or mind. Everything is negative because the world of senses must pass through this depressed energy before it gets to your consciousness.

When you work on this blocked energy, thinking about something that triggers it, you stimulate the samskara, and it opens like a flower and begins to release the stored energy. Suddenly, flashes of what you experienced when an original event took place rush into your consciousness—the thoughts, feelings, and sometimes even smells and other sensory input. You can actually feel the fears and insecurity of a five-year-old when you are much older. This sensation is part of the unfinished mental and emotional energy patterns you have stored and need to process and let go of.

When old heart energies come back up because you were unable to process them before, let go of them now. Once you sit deeply enough inside to stop fighting the stored energy patterns, they will come up and pass right through you. Your heart will become accustomed to releasing and cleansing. Just let it all happen. Get it over with. Stay centered behind them, and let go; the natural flow of your energy will purge the stored patterns from your heart. Then, to achieve the state of an open heart, simply allow new experiences of life to come in and pass through your being.

If you just relax and release, this purification of your heart can be a wonderful thing. Meanwhile, set your eyes on the highest state you can imagine, and don't take them off. If you slip, it doesn't matter; get back up. The fact that you even want to go through this process of freeing energy flow means you are great. Just keep letting go.

Sometimes it is necessary to work on these block energies in therapy. The work in therapy is to understand and then let go and release these persistent blockages. When that is done, you are free. You will have chosen to live a life with an open heart and will experience feelings of love and acceptance.

Doing this work—either outside or in therapy—will enable you to enjoy life instead of clinging to it or pushing it away. When you are able to live with an open heart, each moment will change you. When you are able to experience the gift of life instead of fighting with it, you will be moved to the depth of your being. When you reach this state, you will begin to see the secrets of the heart. The heart is the place through which energy flows to sustain you. This energy inspires you and raises you. It is the strength that carries you through life. It is the beautiful experience of love that pours through your whole being. Opening your heart and letting love in is what this state is about.

The highest state you have ever experienced is simply the result of how open you were. If you don't close, life can be like that all the time. Don't sell yourself short. This unending feeling of inspiration, love, and openness can go on all of the time. That is the natural state of a healthy heart.

Conclusion

Creating Your Best Life

Freedom is our capacity to take a
hand in our own development.
It is our capacity to mold ourselves.

—Rollo May

How Jon Created His Best Life

Clearing his mind of the old stories was a powerful step for Jon. He also shared with me that what helped him the most was focusing on love and spirituality. Learning the spiritual path was a liberating experience for him. Keeping his heart open in all situations of life and being grateful and loving became key points for Jon.

Here is how Jon described his own experience of personal growth that occurred through our work together:

I have so much to share. I have been with you now for a year and my life has truly changed. I have been keeping a journal. I realize that I've worked hard and did the work and want to share it with you.

Mind: It started with my understanding of how I was creating my analogies and stories and thoughts of myself and they were so confusing. I realized with your guidance that when I was younger my love and my passion was for fixing motorcycles, doing creative things, loving and experiencing nature. I was ecstatic when I was in the ocean surfing. There was a part of me that wanted to do something to help the world, and I knew this at a deep level but never discussed it or told anyone about it. But the negativity… I grew up with a lot of self-criticism, self-loathing. I was not good enough; there was a lack of self-love, along with tension and stress to try to be the best. I spent time with you cleaning up these old blockages, clarifying my understanding of who I was, and canceling the pity party. Opening my heart to the world and myself was the beginning of this journey, letting go of the frustration and anger I held. Forgiving and loving.

Body: I then worked with the Biofeedback to reduce the tension and stress I was putting on myself. I now own what I was doing to myself— first with the things I was telling myself and second with how I allowed it to affect my body. As I learned mindful breathing and relaxation, I was able to let go of the stress this inner dialogue was placing on me. My headaches and stomach problems and sleep problems have left me. I've learned how to self-regulate and become resilient and calm myself down. My body is more connected to me, and I have a calm mind and calm body. This is fabulous! Never felt so connected to my inner being.

Brain: With the Neurofeedback, I was able to regulate the brain activity and regulate the neurocircuitry of the brain. I especially liked the alpha theta treatment aspect, which in turn helped me focus on my meditation and the inner work that I needed to complete. So now when I meditate, I can access that deep calm within me.

Spirituality: I am aware of the wonder of Nature and the rapture of the outdoor experiences that I have added to my life. I am able to share this with my family and my wife and children and that harmony of my chakra energy permeates all that I do, all that I say, and all of my life. I have learned to self-regulate my state of being and create my best life with all the choices I make. I am fully awake and aware and have the clarity and the freedom to choose my best life. I fully understand who it is that I am and finally can be fully me.

Love: Yes, Love is the answer. The Beatles had it right. The poetry of Rumi is such a part of my daily meditation and expression of who I am and how I feel. I have never in my life experienced the rapture and completeness of this feeling having my heart open and touched by my everyday experiences.

I feel such love in my heart; my heart is open as
it has never been in my life. I feel your open heart,
Dr. Lita, and that has helped me get to where I am.
You have modeled that for me.

Jon then expressed how important it had been for me to share
stories and experiences of my own and of others in his therapy
sessions. Correspondingly, the discussion of the importance of
storytelling in psychology and medicine has grown recently, as
evidenced in the *New York Times* piece "Why Doctors Need
Stories" by Peter D. Kramer, a psychiatrist and the author of
Listening to Prozac. In response to the case stories in his book,
readers wrote to say that the examples had helped them recognize
issues in themselves or in their loved ones. The stories had also
given them hope. Kramer noted, too, that his professors' stories of
encounters with patients continue to inform his own work with
clients.

In writing about his experience with storytelling in therapy,
Jon wrote the following:

First, Dr. Lita I want to thank you very much for
all that you do. I am so appreciative of our sessions,
and I want to reiterate my amazement at your use
of storytelling. I came away from our session with
a new vision of your power as a therapist, which is
to weave your patient's issues into stories reflecting
your own experiences in life and those of others. I
am now convinced that the traditional philosophy
that the therapist should just listen and should
never personalize is archaic and outmoded and that

when a therapist like you brings decades of world experience, it is a rich resource to use in creating a framework for the client-patient to process their own issues.

In your own personal journey of creating your best life, stay open to learning from the stories and experiences of others. If you seek out a therapist, find one with an approach that includes storytelling (likely a cognitive behavior therapist). If you are working on yourself outside of therapy, remember to keep journaling to capture your feelings and experiences. Also, share what you're learning with a close friend or two whom you trust, and listen to their stories. Consider joining a support group for further sharing and growth.

The Secret of Unconditional Happiness

The highest spiritual path is living life itself. If you know how to live daily life, opening up and embracing life becomes a liberating experience. But first, you have to approach life properly, or it can be confusing. To begin with, you have to realize that you only have one choice in this life, and it's not about your career, which person you want to marry, or whether you want to seek God. People tend to burden themselves with many choices, but in the end, you can throw it all away and make one basic, underlying decision: Do you want to be happy, or do you not want to be happy? It is that simple. Once you make that choice, your path through life becomes clear.

Most people don't dare give themselves that choice, because they think happiness is not under their control. Someone might say, "Well, of course I want to be happy, but my wife left me." In other words, that person wants to be happy, but not if his wife leaves him. But that was not the question. The question was simply "Do you want to be happy or not?" If you keep it that simple, you'll see that the answer is under your control. Believing otherwise happens because you have deep-seated preferences that get in the way.

For instance, let's say that you have been lost and without food for days, and you finally find your way to a house. You can hardly make it to the doorstep, but you manage to pull yourself up and knock on the door. Somebody opens the door, looks at you, and says, "Oh my God! You poor thing! Do you want something to eat? What would you like?" Now, the truth is, you don't care what that person gives you. You don't even want to think about it. You just utter the word *food*. And because you really mean it when you say you need food, your desire no longer has anything to do with your mental preferences. The same goes for the question about happiness. The question is simply "Do you want to be happy?" If the answer is yes, then say it without qualifying it. After all, what the question really means is "Do you want to be happy from this point forward for the rest of your life, regardless of what happens?"

Now, if you say yes, it might happen that your wife leaves you, or your husband dies, or the stock market crashes, or your car breaks down on an open highway at night. Those things might happen between now and the end of your life. But if you want to walk the highest spiritual path, then when you answer yes to that simple question, you must really mean it. No ifs, ands, or buts about it. You see, it's not a question of whether your happiness is under your control—of course it is under your control. It's just that you don't really mean it when you say you're willing to stay happy. You want to qualify that statement. You want to say that as long as this or that does or does not happen, then you are willing to be happy. This self-imposed restriction is why it seems as if happiness is out of your control. Any condition you create will limit your happiness. You are not going to be able to control things and keep them the way you want them.

You have to give an unconditional answer. If you decide you are going to be happy from now on for the rest of your life, you will not only be happy but also become enlightened. Unconditional happiness is the highest spiritual technique there is. You don't have to learn Sanskrit or read any scriptures. You don't have to renounce the world. You just have to mean it when you say that you choose to be happy—and you have to mean it regardless of what happens. This is truly a spiritual path, and it is as direct and sure a path to awakening as could possibly exist.

Once you decide you want to be unconditionally happy, something inevitably will happen that challenges you. This test of your commitment is exactly what stimulates spiritual growth. In fact, it is the unconditional aspect of your commitment that makes this the highest path. It's simple. You just have to decide whether or not you will break your vow. When everything is going well, it's easy to be happy, but the moment something difficult happens, it's not so easy. You tend to find yourself saying, "But I didn't know this was going to happen," "I didn't think I would miss my flight," or "I didn't think Caroline would show up at the party wearing the same dress that I had on." Are you willing to break your vow of happiness because these events took place?

Billions of things could happen that you have not even thought of yet. The question is not whether they will happen, because things are definitely going to happen! The question is whether you want to be happy regardless of what happens. The purpose of your life is to enjoy and learn from your experiences. You're not helping anybody or yourself by being miserable. You were born, and you're going to die. During the time in between, you get to choose whether or not you want to enjoy the experience. Events do not determine whether or not you're going to be happy. They're just situations. You're the one who determines whether or not you're going to be happy. You can be happy just to be alive. If you can live this way, your heart will be open, and your spirit will be free. You will feel yourself soar up to the heavens!

This path leads you to absolute transcendence, because any part of your being that would add a condition to your commitment to happiness has got to go. If you want to be happy, you have to let go of the part of you that wants to create melodrama. That is the part that thinks there is a reason not to be happy, the part that has no self-love. Well, when you transcend the personal, you will naturally awaken to the higher aspects of your being.

In the end, enjoying life's experiences is the only rational thing to do. You're sitting on a planet spinning around in the middle of nowhere. You're floating in empty space in a universe that goes on forever. If you have to be here, at least be happy and enjoy the experience. You're going to die anyway. Things are going to happen anyway. Why shouldn't you be happy?

This choice to enjoy life will lead you through your spiritual journey. In truth, this choice is itself the spiritual teacher. Committing yourself to unconditional happiness will teach you every single thing there is to learn about yourself, others, and the nature of life. You'll learn all about your mind, heart, and will. Just enjoy the life that comes to you. Every time a part of you begins to get unhappy, let it go. Stay open; use affirmations.

The key to staying happy begins by understanding your inner energies. When you look inside, you'll see that when you're happy, your heart feels open, and the energy rushes up inside of you. When you're not happy, your heart closes up. So to stay happy, don't close your heart. No matter what happens, stay open. Don't let the slightest thing, such as someone cutting you off on the freeway and upsetting you, make you unhappy for the rest of the day. What good comes from letting a single incident ruin your day? There is no benefit. Let it go, and stay open.

Taking this path of unconditional happiness takes us through various stages. You stay conscious, centered, and committed at all times. You will have to stay one-pointed on your commitment to remain open and receptive to life. The great masters taught us that God is joy, God is ecstasy, and God is love. If you remain open, waves of uplifting energy will fill your heart. Spiritual practices are not an end; they bear fruit when you become deep enough and remain open. The key is to learn to keep your mind disciplined so that it does not trick you into thinking that you have to close down. If you slip, get back up. The minute you slip and start to close off, pick yourself up and affirm inwardly that you don't want to close down, no matter what happens. You want to be at peace and appreciate your life. If you have trouble remembering, then meditate. Meditation strengthens your center of consciousness so that you're always aware and will not close your heart. Relax your heart when it starts to tighten. You don't have to be outwardly glowing all the time; you are joyful inside. Instead of complaining, you're having fun with the different situations that unfold.

Unconditional happiness is a high path and a high technique because it solves everything. You could learn yoga techniques, such as meditation and postures, but what do you do with the rest of your life? The technique of unconditional happiness is ideal because what you're doing with the rest of your life is already defined: you're letting go of yourself so that you can remain happy. Individuals who actually do this every moment of every day are going to notice the cleansing of the heart, because they're not getting involved in the situations that come up. They're not getting involved in the mind's melodrama. They will come to know a happiness that is beyond human understanding.

View your spiritual work as learning to live a life of love without stress, problems, fear, or melodrama. This path of using life to evolve spiritually is truly the highest path. If you choose to live life this way, you'll see that you can live life in a state of love, happiness, and inner peace.

A Gift to Bring You

by Rumi

You have no idea how hard I've looked
For a gift to bring you.
Nothing seemed right.
What's the point of bringing gold to
The gold mine, or water to the ocean.
Everything I came up with was like
Taking spices to the Orient.
It's no good giving my heart and my
Soul because you already have these.
So I've brought you a mirror.
Look at yourself and remember me.

Bibliography

Benson, Herbert. *The Relaxation Response.* New York: William Morrow, 1975.

Benson, Herbert. *Timeless Healing: The Power and Biology of Belief.* New York: Scribner, 1996.

Borysenko, Joan. *Minding the Body, Mending the Mind.* New York: Bantam Books, 1988.

Brown, Barbara B. *Between Health and Illness.* New York: Bantam Books, 1984.

Budzynski, T. H. "Feedback Induced Muscle Relaxation: Applications to Tension Headache." *Journal of Behavior Therapy and Experimental Psychiatry* 1 (1970): 1–14.

Engel, George L. "The Need for a New Medical Model: A Challenge for Biomedicine." *Science* 196 (1977): 129–136.

Fanning, Patrick. *Visualization for Change.* Oakland: New Harbinger Publications, 1988.

Frankl, Viktor. *Man's Search for Meaning.* Boston: Beacon Press, 2006.

Fuller, George D. *Biofeedback: Methods and Procedures in Clinical Practice.* San Francisco: Biofeedback Press, 1977.

Gawain, Shakti. *Creative Visualization.* Berkeley: Whatever Publications, 1978.

Green, Elmer E. "Voluntary Control of Internal States." *Journal of Transpersonal Psychology* 2 (1970): 1–26.

Green, Elmer E. "Feedback Techniques for Deep Relaxation." *Psychophysiology* 6, no. 3 (1970): 371–377.

Green, Judith Alyce, and Robert Shellenberger. *The Dynamics of Health and Wellness: A Biopsychosocial Approach.* Fort Worth: Holt, Rhinehart, and Winston, 1991.

Horner, Althea J. *Being and Loving.* New Jersey: Aronson, 1978.

Jacobsen, Edmund. *Progressive Relaxation.* Chicago: University of Chicago Press, 1928.

Jacobsen, Edmund. *Progressive Relaxation.* Chicago: University of Chicago Press, 1938.

Jacobsen, Walter E. *Forgive to Win!* Create Space, 2010.

Jung, C. G. *Archetypes of the Collective Unconscious.* New Jersey: Princeton Press, 1968.

Kabat-Zinn, Jon. *Full Catastrophe Living.* New York: Delacorte Press, 1990.

Kohli, Daniel. *Muscle Relaxation and Dysponses* (1974).

Kramer, Peter D. "Why Doctors Need Stories." *New York Times,* October 18, 2014.

Meichenbaum, Donald. *A Clinical Handbook.* Waterloo: Institute Press, 1994.

Miller, Neal E. "Learning of Visceral and Glandular Responses." *Science* 163 (1969): 434–445.

Mercier, Patricia. *The Chakra Bible.* New York: Sterling, 2007.

Padesky, Christine, and Dennis Greenberg. *Mind over Mood: Change How You Feel by Changing the Way You Think.* New York: Guilford Press, 1995.

Pelletier, Kenneth R. *Sound Mind, Sound Body: A New Model for Lifelong Health.* New York: Simon and Schuster, 1994.

Seligman, Martin. *Authentic Happiness.* New York: Random House, 2002.

Seligman, Martin. *Learned Optimism.* New York: Knopf, 1991.

Selye, Hans. *Stress and Disease.* 1956.

Shultz, J. Luthe. *Autogenic Training Methods.* New York: Grune and Stratton, 1967.

Tolle, Ekhart. *The Power of Now.* Novato, CA: New World Library, 1999.

Tolle, Ekhart. *Stillness Speaks.* Novato, CA: New World Library, 2003.

Zi, Nancy. *The Art of Breathing.* New York: Bantam Books, 1986.

About the Authors

Lita Rawdin Singer, PhD, is a professor, psychologist, author, and musician, as well as a fine-art photographer. She has traveled extensively, leading professional study tours to China eight times, Tibet twice, Nepal, Africa, Russia, South America, Turkey, India, Indonesia, Bali, Thailand, Singapore, Riga (Latvia), Estonia, Australia, New Zealand, and throughout Europe.

Her first career was as a stockbroker, and she worked as one of the first women on Wall Street. She earned her BA and MA at California University, Northridge, and her doctorate in psychology at California Graduate Institute. She received the Distinguished Professor Award in 1990 and 2000.

Dr. Singer's three decades as a professor and in clinical practice working with individuals, couples, and families have given her the practical experience and the knowledge to understand what's missing for people, and she is able to guide them to become physically, mentally, emotionally, and spiritually healthy. She commits her life to teaching these skills.

www.drlita.com
www.biofeedbacktreatmentcenter.com
www.adamwastrappedevewasframed.com

Stephanie Dawn Singer, MS (marriage and family therapist intern #69285), is a biofeedback and neurofeedback therapist specializing in applied psychophysiology. She specializes in mindful cognitive therapy for individuals, couples, families, and children. She uses both neurofeedback and biofeedback as adjuncts for her clients.

She has been using biofeedback to treat anxiety, depression, attention deficits, stress-related issues, and other mind-body symptoms, such as migraines, tinnitus, temporomandibular joint dysfunction, and sleep disorders.

Stephanie's experience in China in 1985 allowed her to see the Chinese concept of preventive medicine, focusing on treatment of the whole person to become and stay healthy. Like her mother, Dr. Singer, Stephanie believes that mind, body, soul, and spirit are the core of helping people to find their inner peace and mind-body harmony.

Brandon Louis Singer, BA, is a graduate student pursuing his master's degree in marriage and family therapy. He has been working with the techniques and skills of biofeedback at the Biofeedback and Neurofeedback Treatment Center as an adjunct to the work he is doing with patients utilizing mindful cognitive behavioral therapy. He works with individuals, couples, families, and children. Like Stephanie and his grandmother, Dr. Singer, Brandon seeks to treat the whole person—mind, body, soul, and spirit.

The Biofeedback and Neurofeedback Treatment Center

22055 Clarendon Street, Suite 106
Woodland Hills, CA 91367
818-992-9300

This book is based on the integrative treatment model we use at the Biofeedback and Neurofeedback Treatment Center in Woodland Hills, California. The treatment model we utilize incorporates a biopsychosocial-spiritual approach. We also use cognitive behavioral techniques, which help clients understand their behavior and teach them new behaviors, new options, and how to gain control of their lives as they begin to see that they have choices.

When someone is traumatized as a child through physical or emotional injury, his or her mind and body create and develop certain response patterns. Since the brain and the body naturally desire balance, the biofeedback and neurofeedback merely assist in bringing the client back into balance.

Biofeedback and neurofeedback are the most-compelling examples of the brain and the body's ability to learn to self-regulate and bring themselves back into balance. These technologies offer individuals an opportunity to participate in their own healing process.

Biofeedback allows the body responses of muscle tension, blood flow, and galvanic skin response to be amplified and projected on a computer screen as they are occurring in the body. This enables a skilled and precise interpretation of the body responses and provides the opportunity for immediate correction of these responses. The effect of biofeedback training is similar to the effect of training wheels on a bicycle. Once a client learns to balance by her- or himself, the training wheels are no longer needed. The body does not forget.

Neurofeedback addresses the problems of brain dysregulation. During neurofeedback, we use the latest technology to train a client's brain to correct the faulty brain-wave activity. You can think of neurofeedback as brain exercise. Like a muscle, your brain gets stronger the more you train it. Since your brain controls every nerve system, muscle, and organ in your body, when it works at maximum efficiency, you feel better and perform better.

Note: It is imperative that when you decide to use these adjunct treatments, you get a licensed therapist, not just a technician, as your practitioner. We have been using biofeedback as an adjunct to therapy for more than thirty years. We have added neurofeedback so that clients can benefit from the cutting-edge revolution in psychology that is being driven by the innovations in neuroscientific research. Integrating neuroscientific and psychotherapeutic treatments is the most-effective path to psychological healing and growth, because the two approaches work synergistically to create a brain state this is most receptive to treatment.

For more information, contact the following:

Dr. Lita Rawdin Singer, Clinical Director
The Biofeedback and Neurofeedback Treatment Center
Licensed Clinical Psychologist, Researcher, and Professor
www.biofeedbacktreatmentcenter.com
www.drlita.com
drlitasinger@cox.net

Book Dr. Lita as a Speaker or Media Guest

If you're interested in booking Dr. Lita Singer, PhD, as a speaker, then you're invited to call her at the office at 818-992-9300 or 805-965-7033 or to contact her by e-mail at drlitasinger@ cox.net. Dr. Singer has taught undergraduate and graduate college classes, as well as leading popular community workshops and traveling all over the world while leading study groups for mental-health professionals.

Dr. Singer is also available for media interviews.